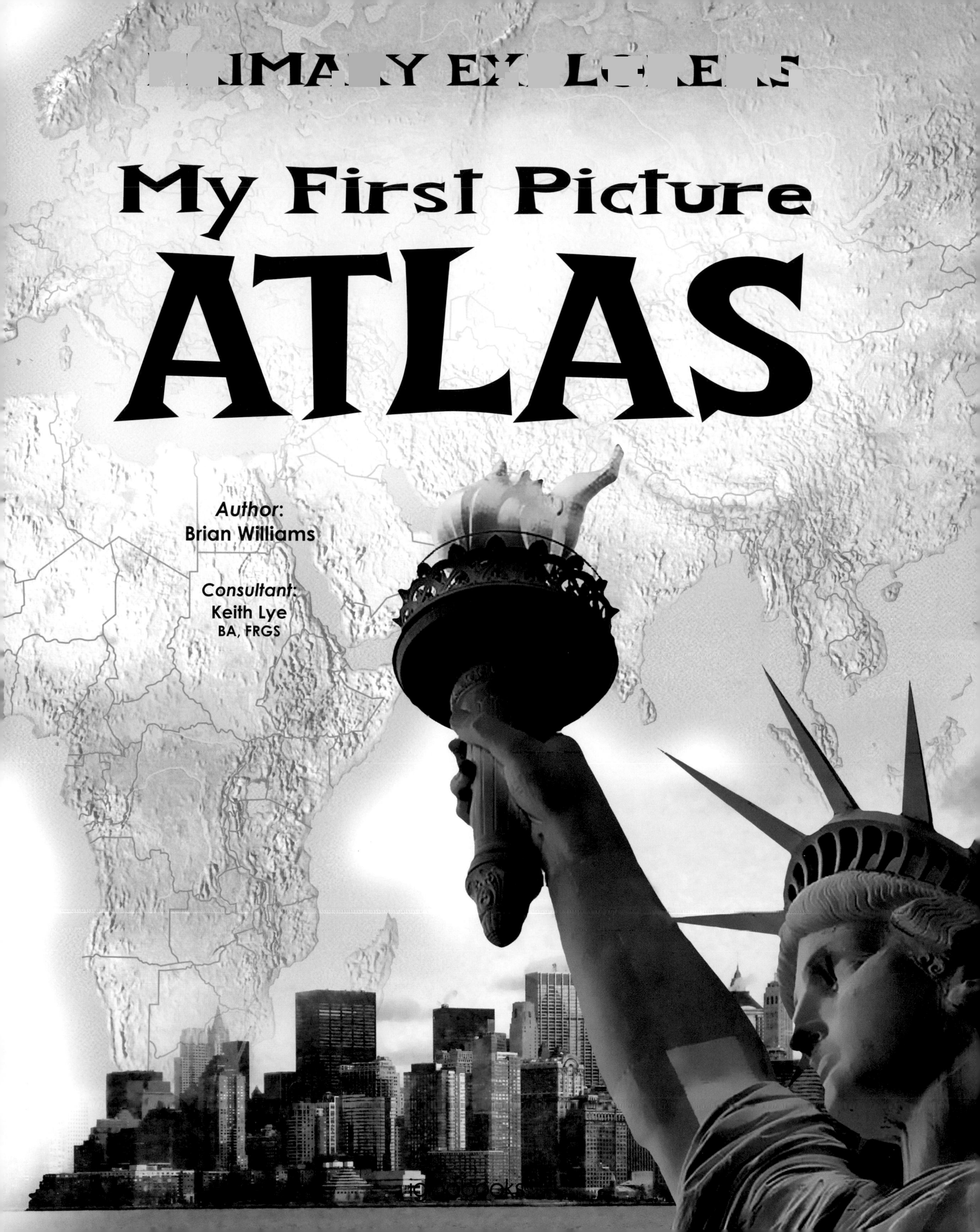

PRIMARY EXPLORERS

My First Picture
ATLAS

Author:
Brian Williams

Consultant:
Keith Lye
BA, FRGS

CONTENTS

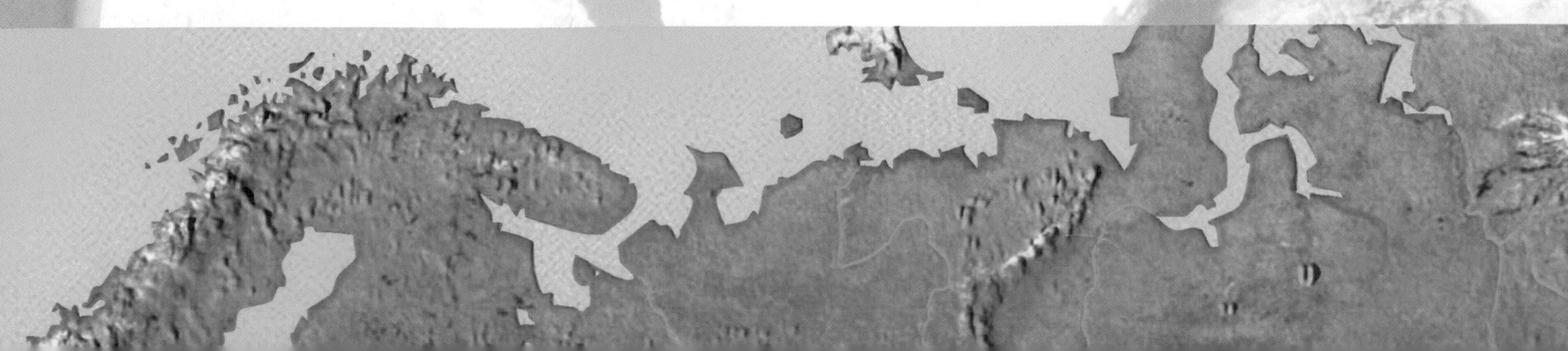

HOW TO USE THIS ATLAS

Maps show our world in a way that helps us find places and understand natural features.

An atlas is a book of maps. This atlas is divided into regions, each of which has a map. The key on the right will help you use the maps. There is information about each region's climate and landscape, followed by information about its people, places, plants and animals. Look out, too, for the 'Did You Know?' boxes and the list of 'Outstanding Sights' for each region.

BOX FEATURES

The box features in this book are picture-panels containing specific information about various subjects. They might be about a country, such as New Zealand or Russia, or local wildlife, such as Australasia's unique marsupial animals. These features provide extra information about each atlas region.

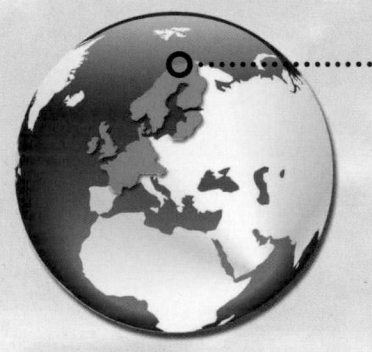

Locator globes show planet Earth as it looks from space. For each region in this atlas, a locator globe shows you where the region is in relation to the rest of the world. It locates the region on the planet.

Famous places, such as the Taj Mahal in India (shown here), are pictured, and you can read about them in the captions next to each picture.

N

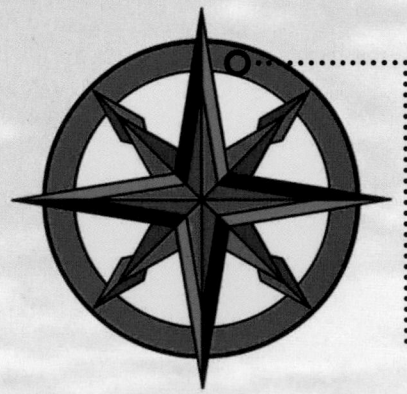

A compass icon next to each map shows you where north is. On a magnetic compass, the needle always points to magnetic north (confusingly not the same as geographical north).

0   Miles   1000

0   Kilometres   1000

Scale bars on maps indicate distances. On this scale bar, miles are on the upper bar and kilometres on the lower bar. All maps are drawn to a scale: for example, 1: 2,000,000 means 1 unit of distance on the map equals 2 million units on the ground.

Animal and plant life varies from region to region. Illustrations show wildlife typical of the Earth's environments. Each species has its own 'ecological niche' in nature.

Physical features, such as mountains, deserts and lakes, shape the landscape of each region and affect the way local people live.

MAP KEY

Lakes are large bodies of inland fresh water. Large lakes are named.

Mountains are shown in relief (they appear to stand out). The highest are shown as snow-coverd.

Large islands are shown and named, in their oceans or seas.

Coastline surrounds each land mass. Seas and oceans are shown in blue.

States in the United States, and provinces in Canada, are named like this.

Cities are shown by a black dot, with the name alongside.

Country names are shown in large capital letters.

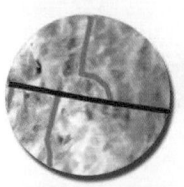

State and province borders (USA and Canada) are shown as orange lines. **Country borders** are shown as red lines.

Rivers are shown in blue, and important rivers are named.

BRITISH COLUMBIA

ALBERTA

MANITOBA

Peace

SASKATCHEWAN

Prince Rupert

Athabasca

N. Saskatchewan

Edmonton

Saskatoon

Calgary

S. Saskatchewan

Vancouver

Regina

Seattle
Olympia

WASHINGTON

Missouri

NORTH DAKOTA

Bismarck

Salem

Helena

MONTANA

SOUTH DAKOTA

St.

Boise

Pierre

OREGON IDAHO

WYOMING

Missouri

Platte NEBRASKA

Sacramento

Carson City

Salt Lake City

Cheyenne

Lincoln

San Francisco

NEVADA

UTAH

Colorado

Denver

COLORADO

Topeka

Arkansas KANSAS

Las Vegas

UNITED STATES O AMERICA

CALIFORNIA

Los Angeles

ARIZONA

Santa Fe

Canadian

OKLAHOM

Oklahoma C

Red

San Diego

Phoenix

NEW MEXICO

TEXAS

Dallas

El Paso

Colorado

Aus

PACIFIC OCEAN

Hermosillo

Rio Grande

San Antonio

Chihuahua

MEXICO

1 **A yellow dot** shows the location of a subject featured on the *Climate and landscape* pages.

2 **A red dot** shows the location of a subject featured on the *People, places, plants and animals* pages.

Torreón

Monterrey

Tamp

MEXICO

PLANET EARTH

The Earth is a planet. It orbits the Sun, which is a medium-sized star.

The Earth is a sphere (a ball), slightly flattened at the poles. It is a rocky world, mostly covered with water (the oceans) separating land masses (the continents), and with an atmosphere of gases. Life on Earth thrives because it has air and water, and is neither too hot nor too cold. People are changing the Earth by cutting down its forests, and they are using energy in ways that increase 'global warming,' which is affecting the climate.

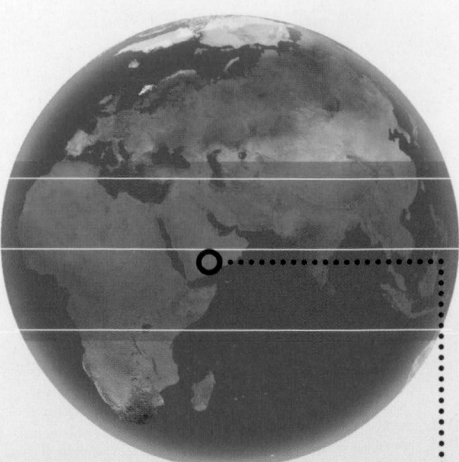

Tropic of Cancer
23° 27' N

Equator
0° latitude

Tropic of Capricorn
23° 27' S

The Tropics and the Equator are shown on maps. The Equator is an imaginary line around the middle of the Earth. The Tropics are two imaginary lines to the north and south of the Equator. They are the boundaries of the region known as the tropical or equatorial zone.

THE EARTH AND THE SUN

The Earth's climate and seasons are governed by the Sun, which gives off vast amounts of energy. Earth's atmosphere acts like a heat shield. Lands nearer the Equator are warmer, because the Sun is directly overhead. At the Poles, the Sun's rays have further to travel through the atmosphere, so the polar climates are colder. The seasons change as the Earth shows different sides to the Sun during its orbit.

The Milky Way galaxy contains millions of stars, one of which is our Sun. There are countless other galaxies in the Universe.

The Earth is one of eight planets orbiting the Sun. From the Sun they are: Mercury, Venus, Earth, Mars, Jupiter, Saturn, Uranus and Neptune. Tiny Pluto is no longer regarded as a planet.

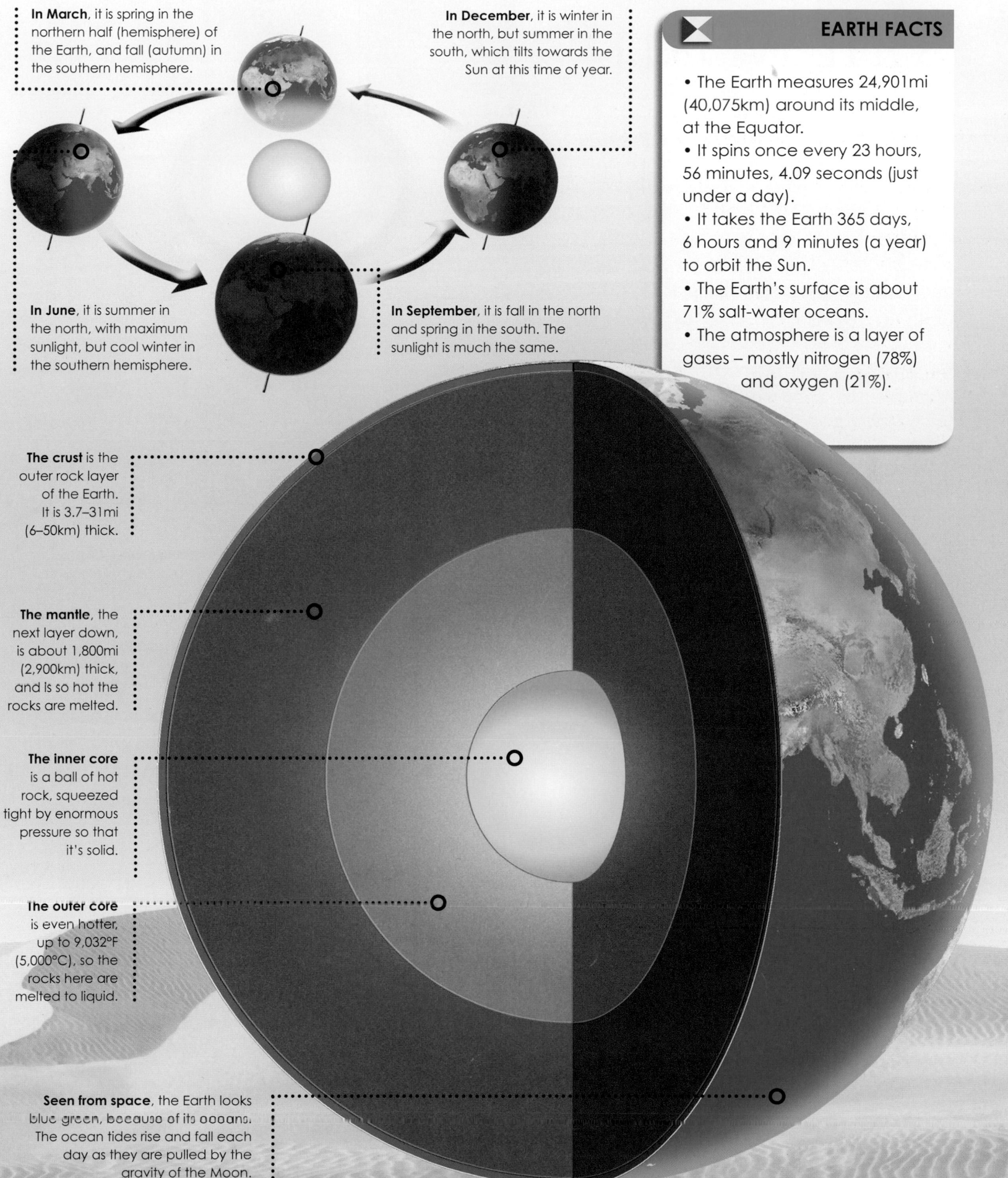

In March, it is spring in the northern half (hemisphere) of the Earth, and fall (autumn) in the southern hemisphere.

In December, it is winter in the north, but summer in the south, which tilts towards the Sun at this time of year.

In June, it is summer in the north, with maximum sunlight, but cool winter in the southern hemisphere.

In September, it is fall in the north and spring in the south. The sunlight is much the same.

EARTH FACTS

• The Earth measures 24,901mi (40,075km) around its middle, at the Equator.
• It spins once every 23 hours, 56 minutes, 4.09 seconds (just under a day).
• It takes the Earth 365 days, 6 hours and 9 minutes (a year) to orbit the Sun.
• The Earth's surface is about 71% salt-water oceans.
• The atmosphere is a layer of gases – mostly nitrogen (78%) and oxygen (21%).

The crust is the outer rock layer of the Earth. It is 3.7–31mi (6–50km) thick.

The mantle, the next layer down, is about 1,800mi (2,900km) thick, and is so hot the rocks are melted.

The inner core is a ball of hot rock, squeezed tight by enormous pressure so that it's solid.

The outer core is even hotter, up to 9,032°F (5,000°C), so the rocks here are melted to liquid.

Seen from space, the Earth looks blue-green, because of its oceans. The ocean tides rise and fall each day as they are pulled by the gravity of the Moon.

THE WORLD

The map of the world looks familiar, but in fact the Earth is constantly changing.

Earth's outer layer of rock, the crust, supports the planet's continents and oceans. Because the crust rests on very hot molten rocks deep inside the Earth, the continents are continually moving and colliding with each other.

THE SEVEN CONTINENTS

A continent is a large mass of land. The Earth has seven continents, shown on the big map. Millions of years ago, these land masses were joined up, forming a huge 'super-continent' called Pangaea. The oceans separate the continents, though North America is joined to South America by a narrow strip of land, and Europe is joined to Asia.

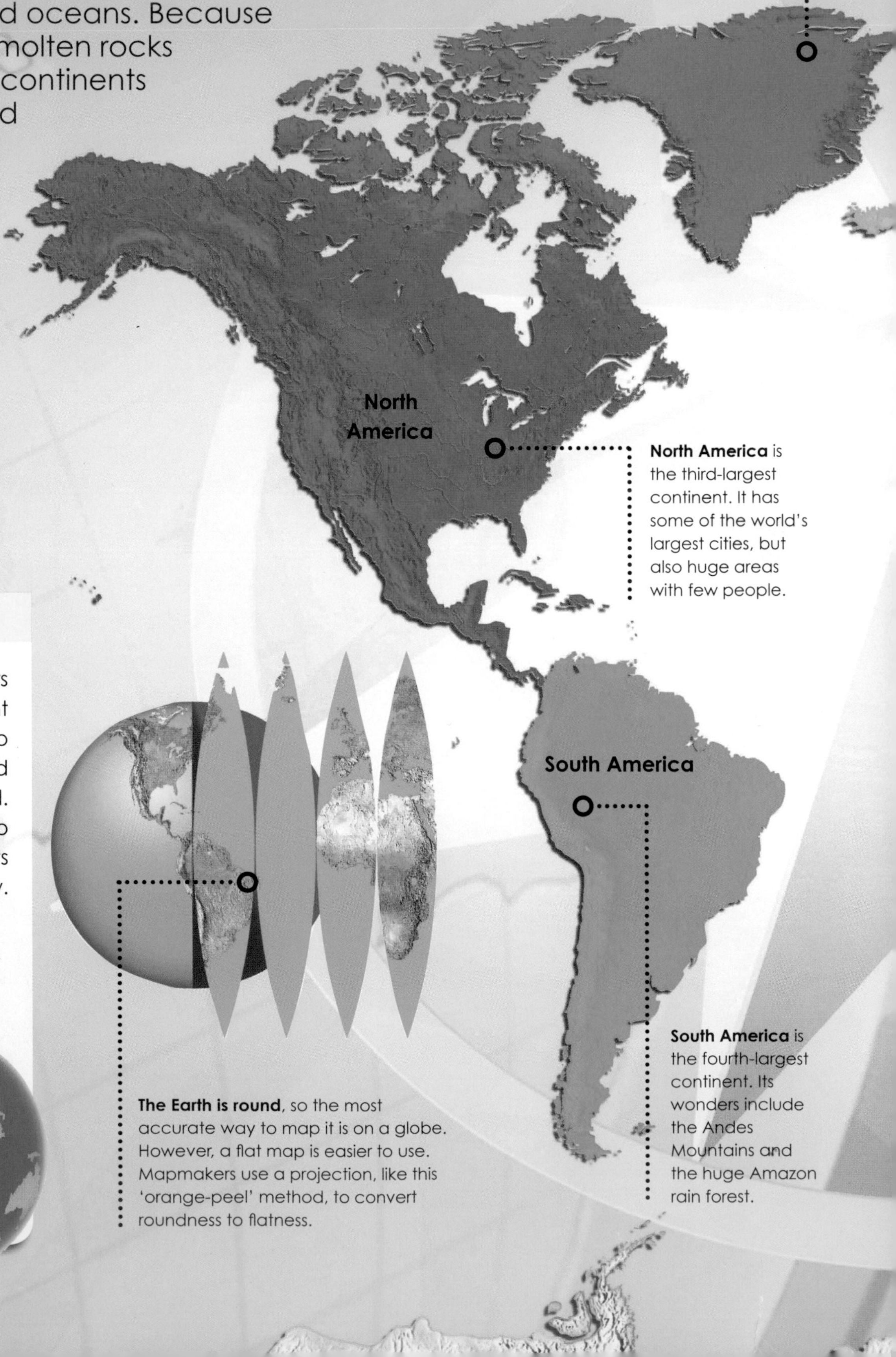

Greenland is the world's biggest island, excluding Australia. Geographically part of North America, it's a dependency of Denmark.

North America

North America is the third-largest continent. It has some of the world's largest cities, but also huge areas with few people.

South America

South America is the fourth-largest continent. Its wonders include the Andes Mountains and the huge Amazon rain forest.

CONTINENTAL DRIFT

Super-continent

About 180 million years ago, the super-continent of Pangaea split into two: Laurasia and Gondwanaland. They drifted apart to form the continents of today.

Breaking apart

Still drifting

The Earth is round, so the most accurate way to map it is on a globe. However, a flat map is easier to use. Mapmakers use a projection, like this 'orange-peel' method, to convert roundness to flatness.

Longitude lines on a map are drawn from north to south. The prime meridian (0° longitude) runs through Greenwich, in London (UK).

Latitude lines are drawn from east to west. The Equator, the imaginary line around the middle of the Earth, is the line of 0° latitude.

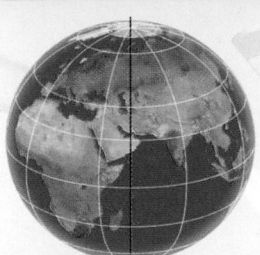

Degrees are units; a circle has 360 degrees (°). Latitude and longitude lines are marked in degrees, to pinpoint any grid location.

Asia is the largest continent. It has more than half the world's people.

Asia

Europe

CLIMATE AND VEGETATION

Climate is the average weather of a place. Tropical areas are mostly hotter than regions nearer to the Poles. Altitude also affects climate: temperatures fall about 3.5°F every 1,000ft (6°C for every 1,000m) of altitude. Nearness to the ocean affects climate, because water retains heat longer than land. That's why extreme climates are found in the middle of continents. Climate affects vegetation, too. About 25% of the Earth's land surface is covered in forest, and about 20% is hot desert. About 10% is ice-covered.

Africa

Europe comes sixth in order of size (only Australasia is smaller), but ranks second in population after Asia.

Australasia

Africa is the second-largest continent. Its shape suggests it was once joined to South America.

Antarctica is the only continent that has no native people. It is too cold and barren.

Australasia or Oceania includes Australia, New Zealand and surrounding islands in the Pacific Ocean. Much of Australia is empty desert.

Antarctica

NORTH AMERICA

Climate and landscape

North America is the third-biggest continent on Earth. The landscape includes icy polar regions, high mountains, flat grasslands or prairies and dense forests. Amazing natural features of North America include the Grand Canyon and the Rocky Mountains.

THE ICY NORTH

Much of northern Canada, the US state of Alaska, and the island of Greenland (belonging to Denmark) are within the Arctic Circle. On the treeless tundra plains, temperatures rise above freezing for only a few weeks in summer. In winter, it is bitterly cold. Much of the Arctic is frozen sea. Very few people live here; the only native peoples are the Inuit, who learnt to live and hunt for food in this harsh, snowy environment.

Canada, the United States and Mexico make up North America. Although Canada is the biggest country in the region (and the second-biggest in the world), the USA has ten times as many people. Mexico's population (111 million) is four times bigger now than it was in 1960.

NUMBER OF COUNTRIES
3

HIGHEST MOUNTAIN
Mt McKinley in Alaska, USA, 20,320ft (6,194m).

LONGEST RIVER
The Missouri–Mississippi river system, USA, at 3,900mi (6,300km) long.

OUTSTANDING SIGHTS

Hudson Bay, Canada – the world's biggest bay.
Lake Superior, between Canada and the United States – the world's biggest freshwater lake.
Redwoods and sequoias in California, USA – the world's biggest trees.
Mexico City, Mexico – North America's biggest city, with over 18.2 million people (including suburbs).
Washington DC, home to the White House and the Library of Congress (the world's biggest library).
The Metropolitan Museum of Art, New York City, USA.
The Golden Gate Bridge, San Francisco – an engineering marvel.

DID YOU KNOW?

A tornado can toss trucks into the air and tear houses apart. Over land, the tornado forms a spiral dust-cloud; over water, the winds create a tube of water.

1 **Tornadoes** are whirling windstorms that race across the central plains of North America. Americans call them 'twisters.' A tornado creates a huge funnel of whirling air that stretches down to the ground, and travels as fast as a car.

2 **The Grand Canyon** is a gorge cut by the Colorado River. The Canyon is 277mi (446km) long and 18mi (29km) across at its widest point. At its deepest, 1mi (1.6km) down, are rocks that are 2 billion years old!

Barrow

ALASKA (USA)

Yukon

Fairbanks

Anchorage

YUKON TERRITORY

Whitehorse

Juneau

Prince Rupert

Sale

Sacramento

Sa

CALIFOR

PAC OC

3 **The Niagara Falls** are shared between the United States and Canada. The Horseshoe Falls on the Canadian side of the Niagara River are 2,200ft (670m) across. About 85% of the water flows over these falls. The American Falls are a little less wide. The drop to the river is about 188ft (57m).

MOUNTAINS AND DESERTS

The mightiest mountains in North America stretch along the western side of the continent. Here rise the Rocky Mountains, the Sierra Nevada and Sierra Madre. In the east, the main mountains are the Appalachians. In the southwestern United States and northern Mexico are the Mojave Desert, Death Valley and the Sonoran Desert.

Buttes and mesas are rocks shaped by erosion. A mesa has a flat top like a table, and is bigger than a butte.

DID YOU KNOW?

Canada and the United States share the five Great Lakes. Almost 9% of Canada's total area is covered by fresh water.

4 **The desert landscape** of Monument Valley, Utah, has been much-used by film directors. The weird shapes of sandstone rocks have been weathered over millions of years.

NORTH AMERICA

People, places, plants and animals

North America has a fascinating variety of people, landscapes, plants and animals, and is rich in natural resources. Until about 200 years ago, most of the land was wilderness. Modern North America has grown very quickly. The region now has some of the world's biggest cities, and is the most powerful nation in the world.

MELTING POT OF CULTURES

North America's first peoples came from Asia more than 15,000 years ago. They were the ancestors of today's Inuit and Native Americans. Most North Americans have ancestors who came from Europe, Asia, Central and South America or Africa. Many Canadians, for example, are descendants of British and French immigrants. The United States has large African-American and Hispanic (Spanish-speaking) minorities. Many immigrant communities maintain traditions from their homelands, giving the United States a diverse cultural heritage.

WILDLIFE WONDERS

The wildlife of North America includes many large plant-eaters, such as moose, bison (buffalo), caribou, deer and wild sheep. Large predators include bears, mountain lions, jaguars, wolves and alligators. Smaller animals of the forests are beavers, raccoons, skunks and porcupines. The national bird of the United States is the bald eagle. Wildlife is protected in many national parks and game reserves across the region.

THE INUIT

The Inuit of the Arctic traditionally lived by hunting seals and fishing. They made fur clothes, sleds and skin boats, and lived in tents or ice shelters. Many Inuit now do regular jobs, but some still go hunting, using rifles and hand-held harpoons.

5 Mexico has many splendid reminders of the past, when the Olmec, Toltec, Mayan and Aztec civilizations flourished. The Aztecs built pyramid temples, such as this one at Chichen Itza in southern Mexico.

HISPANIC AMERICA

The Spanish explored southwest America in the 1500s, and in 1521 conquered the Aztecs of Mexico. Spain's legacy includes the Catholic Church, architecture and the Spanish language. Mexico is the world's biggest Spanish-speaking country. More than 22 million Hispanic Americans live in the United States.

Alligators live in the swamps of the southeastern USA, where they ambush their prey.

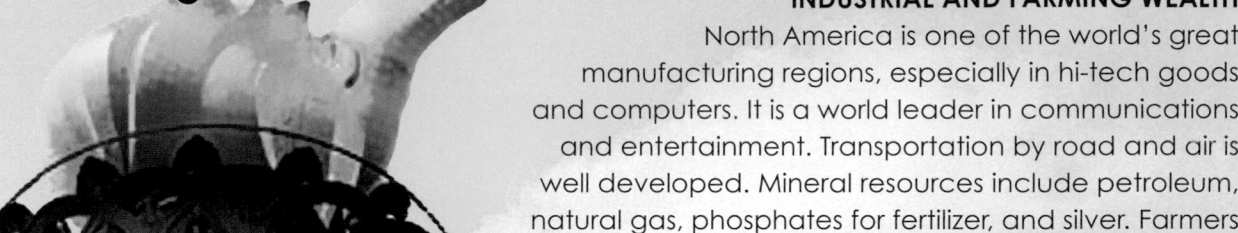

The torch of freedom held by the Statue of Liberty welcomed migrants arriving in America by ship in the late 1800s and early 1900s. The original torch was replaced in 1986 with this copy.

INDUSTRIAL AND FARMING WEALTH

North America is one of the world's great manufacturing regions, especially in hi-tech goods and computers. It is a world leader in communications and entertainment. Transportation by road and air is well developed. Mineral resources include petroleum, natural gas, phosphates for fertilizer, and silver. Farmers grow huge crops of soya beans, grain, cotton and fruits, and raise cattle and sheep on vast ranches. In the warm south are large plantations of bananas, coffee and sugar cane.

The spikes of the crown symbolize heaven's rays shining over the world. The seven rays represent the seven seas and continents of the world.

The Statue of Liberty was given to the United States by France in 1884. The figure is 151ft 1in (46.05 m) tall. Twin stairways wind their way up inside the statue to the crown.

DID YOU KNOW?

Dutch settlers founded New York City in 1626, buying Manhattan Island from the Native Americans for about $24. They called their town New Amsterdam. The English renamed it New York.

6 New York City, USA, is famous for its many high buildings or skyscrapers.

CENTRAL AND SOUTH AMERICA

Climate and landscape

Central America is a narrow strip of land joining North and South America. It has seven independent countries. The Caribbean is an island chain made up of 13 independent nations and many small island territories governed by foreign powers, such as France. South America is 23 times larger in area than Central America and the Caribbean, but its population is only roughly 5 times greater. It has 12 independent countries, the largest being Brazil.

WET AND DRY

Central America is hot all year round, but it has a distinct wet season from June to October, when there is a greater risk of hurricanes. Mid November to May is the dry season. The combination of frequent heavy rain, rivers, mountains and forests make road transport difficult. In South America, the mighty Andes Mountains, which run the length of the west coast, have a big impact on the weather. In the mountains, temperatures can be very cold, and May to November is the driest time of year. The Amazon region, by contrast, is hot and very wet all year round. Patagonia, in the south, is a particularly windy region.

Central America faces the Pacific Ocean to the west and the Atlantic Ocean to the east. At its narrowest point, called the Isthmus of Panama, a canal links the two oceans. To the east lie the islands of the Caribbean Sea, and to the south is the vast region of South America – the world's fourth-largest continent.

NUMBER OF COUNTRIES
32

HIGHEST MOUNTAIN
Mount Aconcagua, Argentina, 22,834ft (6,959m).

LONGEST RIVER
River Amazon, northern South America, 4,000mi (6,400km).

OUTSTANDING SIGHTS

Carnivals in Brazil and the Caribbean.
Aztec temples in Mexico.
Angel Falls, Venezuela – the world's highest waterfall at 3,212ft (979m).
Machu Picchu, Peru – a ruined Inca city.
Lake Titicaca, straddling Bolivia and Peru – the world's highest lake.
The Amazon rain forest, the world's greatest tropical forest with over 40,000 different kinds of plant.
Sugar Loaf Mountain, Rio de Janeiro, Brazil.

Central America is a mountainous region. The highest peak, volcano Tajumulco, rises to 13,845ft (4,220m).

BAHAMAS

ATLANTIC OCEAN

CUBA

JAMAICA HAITI DOMINICAN
REPUBLIC

ANTIGUA &
BARBUDA

PUERTO
RICO

CARIBBEAN
SEA

ST KITTS
& NEVIS

DOMINICA

ST LUCIA

BARBADOS

ST VINCENT & THE
GRENADINES

GRENADA

TRINIDAD
& TOBAGO

Barranquilla

Maracaibo   Caracas   Port of
Spain

PANAMA

Medellín

Bogotá

Cali

COLOMBIA

Quito

ECUADOR

VENEZUELA

Orinoco

GUYANA

Georgetown

SURINAME

Paramaribo

FRENCH GUIANA

Cayenne

Orinoco

Branco

Negro

Macapá

Putumayo

Japurá

Amazon

Manaus

①

Juruá

Purus

Madeira

Tapajós

Xingu

Tocantins

Belèm

São Luis

Fortaleza

PERU

Lima

Marañón

ANDES MOUNTAINS

Lake Titicaca

La Paz

BOLIVIA

Arica

⑥

Manoré

Guaporé

Arinos

Araguaia

BRAZIL

Parnaíba

Recife

São Francisco

Maceió

Salvador

Brasília

**The largest
lake** in the
region is in
Venezuela,
in the
north. Lake
Maracaibo
covers an
area of
5,062sq mi
(13,111sq km).

ATACAMA DESERT

③

CHILE

Santiago

Pilcomayo

PARAGUAY

Asunción

Parana

Salado

Uruguay

Belo Horizonte

São Paulo ④ Rio de Janeiro

Pôrto Alegre

ARGENTINA

Salado

⑤

Rosario

Buenos Aires

URUGUAY

Montevideo

Colorado

Negro

Bahia Blanca

N

② **The Andes
Mountains**
stretch over
4,300mi
(7,000km).
They are
the longest
mountain
range in
the world.

Punta Arenas

Tierra del Fuego

Cape Horn

Chubut

②

**The largest
Caribbean
islands** are
Cuba and
Hispaniola,
which is shared
by Haiti and
the Dominican
Republic.

BAHAMAS

Nassau

Havana

CUBA

DOMINICAN
REPUBLIC

HAITI

Port-Au-Prince

Santo
Domingo

PUERTO
RICO

JAMAICA

Kingston

① **At the heart of the Amazon rain forest** is the
Amazon River, the second-longest river in the
world. The warm, wet forest gets an incredible
108in (274cm) of rain every year! It is home to
millions of plants and animals.

CONTINENT OF CONTRASTS

Many of the mountains in Central America are
active volcanoes, and earthquakes happen fairly
frequently. South America's landscapes vary from
the hot, semi-dry lowlands of the Gran Chaco and
the plains of Argentina to the dense, wet forests of
Brazil and the snow-capped Andes. Mighty rivers
include the Amazon, Orinoco and Rio de la Plata.

| 0 | Miles | 1000 |
| 0 | Kilometres | 1000 |

③ **The Atacama Desert** in
Chile is one of the Earth's
driest places. In some parts,
it may not rain for several
years. The desert is a source
of sodium nitrate, used to
make fertilizers.

CENTRAL AND SOUTH AMERICA

People, places, plants and animals

Central and South America's cultures are a lively mix of Native American, European and African traditions. Most people speak either Spanish or Portuguese, along with local languages. Much of the forest has been cleared for cattle ranches or plantations that grow bananas, coffee and sugar. South America's wildlife includes the slow-moving sloth and the spotted jaguar. Llamas (related to camels) live in the Andes mountains, and rheas (large flightless birds) run across the pampas.

FORESTS AND CITIES

In the Amazon forest, some Native American tribes still live by hunting and food-gathering, as they have for thousands of years, in harmony with nature. However, the modern world is increasingly moving in, bringing airfields, roads, towns and farms. Many poor people have moved to the great cities, such as Río de Janeiro and São Paulo, where shanty slums huddle in the shadow of skyscrapers.

CARIBBEAN REEFS

The coral reefs in the Caribbean Sea attract scuba divers and scientists studying marine life. Coral reefs are a delicate and fragile natural environment, giving shelter and food to many sea creatures.

DID YOU KNOW?

The people of Río de Janeiro are known as Cariocas. Every year, the city stages a spectacular Carnival with four days of dancing and music in the streets.

④ **A giant statue of Jesus Christ** stands on a mountain peak overlooking the bay and city of Río de Janeiro, in Brazil. Christianity was brought to South America by European explorers. Río is one of the chief sea ports in South America.

5 **Gauchos** are South America's cowboys. Expert horsemen, they use their riding skills to round up the cattle and sheep that are raised on large ranches on the grasslands. Some South American farms are enormous – bigger even than some of the world's smaller countries!

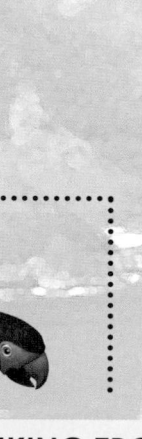

The scarlet macaw is called the 'king of parrots.' Central and South America have many wonderful birds. Sadly, some parrots are now rare, because of hunting, collecting and loss of habitat.

6 **This Bolivian woman** and her baby live in the Andes. European explorers called Native Americans 'Indians.' Life for poor people in South America is often tough, and Indian villagers in the mountains must work hard to survive.

■ SHRINKING TROPICAL RAIN FOREST

Vast areas of forest have been cut down (shown in orange on the map). The trees are being felled by loggers for timber or cleared for mining, farming or to build towns.

Rain forest trees produce products such as nuts, oils and waxes, as well as timber. Many forest plants are used to make medicines, too.

Cutting down trees can cause soil erosion and turn rich forest into wasteland. More than a tenth of the Amazon forest has gone, and more is lost every year. Scientists and local people are campaigning to save this precious natural resource by protecting remaining forest and planting new trees.

Toucan, a rain forest bird

Africa is the second-largest continent. Some of Africa's 53 countries (for example Algeria, Sudan, Nigeria and South Africa) are huge. Others, such as the Seychelles and Gambia, are small. Africa has the world's biggest desert, the Sahara, and the world's longest river, the Nile.

NUMBER OF COUNTRIES
53

HIGHEST MOUNTAIN
Kilimanjaro in Tanzania, 19,340ft (5,895m)

LONGEST RIVER
River Nile, 4,132mi (6,650km)

OUTSTANDING SIGHTS

The pyramids, Egypt – one of the seven wonders of the ancient world.
Victoria Falls, between Zambia and Zimbabwe – Africa's greatest waterfall.
Migrating herds crossing the Serengeti plains, Tanzania.
Table Mountain, overlooking Cape Town, South Africa.
Roman ruins in Libya and Tunisia.
Gorillas and chimpanzees in the forests of West Africa.
The Great Mosque at Djenne in Mali, made of mud bricks.

AFRICA

Climate and landscape

The continent of Africa is such a vast region that it makes up a fifth of the world's land area. It was where the first humans lived millions of years ago. There are still huge areas of unspoilt wilderness, where important habitats and wildlife are protected in national parks from the spread of humans.

STRADDLING THE EQUATOR

Most of Africa lies within the Tropics and is hot. Most countries have two seasons: dry and rainy. Drought is a problem in large areas, and can cause people to starve. There are wide differences in climate and plant life between the deserts of the north (the Sahara) and southwest (the Namib and Kalahari), the rain forests of the west and the savanna grasslands of central Africa.

THE GREAT RIFT VALLEY

The Rift Valley is a crack or fault in the Earth's surface, stretching for some 3,700mi (6,000km) from Syria in western Asia all the way to central Mozambique in eastern Africa. It has some of Africa's richest farmland, and along it are found Africa's Great Lakes, including Lake Victoria, which is 210mi (337km) long.

DID YOU KNOW?

Thousands of years ago, the Sahara was green. Ancient rock paintings in the desert show animals such as hippos and giraffes, now found only on the grasslands further south.

1 **The Sahara Desert** is almost as big as the United States. Most of the Sahara is bare rock, gravel and sand, with just a few oases, or water holes.

2 **The Victoria Falls** on the Zambezi River are 355ft (108m) high. Their African name means 'the smoke that thunders.'

Tangier
Rabat
Casablanca
MOROCCO
ATLAS MOUNTA
ALGERI
El Aaiun
Western Sahara (disputed)
Dakhla
F'Dérik
MAURITANIA
MAL
Nouakchott
Sénégal
Timbuktu
SENEGAL
Dakar
Djenne
GAMBIA
Banjul
Bamako
Ouagadougou
Bissau
BURKINA FA
GUINEA-BISSAU
GUINEA
Babo Dioulasso
Conakry
GHANA
Freetown
IVORY COAST
SIERRA LEONE
Monrovia
Yamoussoukro
TO
LIBERIA
Accra
Abidjan

N

0 Miles 1000
0 Kilometres 1000

3 The River Nile is the world's longest river. It flows north from central Africa into the Mediterranean Sea. Its main tributary, the White Nile, starts from Lake Victoria.

4 Mount Kilimanjaro is a dormant (sleeping) volcano in the east African country of Tanzania. It is close to the Equator, but is snow-covered for most of the year.

Central Africa is covered in rain forest, and is home to rare animals, such as okapis and gorillas.

5 As the Nile nears the Mediterranean, it fans out into a wide delta. This satellite photo shows fertile land (green) with desert all around. The Nile has made civilization possible in Egypt since ancient times.

The island of Madagascar is the only place where lemurs live wild.

TUNISIA
Algiers Annaba
Constantine Tunis
Sfax
Tripoli Misratah
Ghadames Benghazi
Mediterranean Sea
Alexandria
Cairo
Suez
El Faiyum
LIBYA
Libyan Desert
Western Desert
Asyut
Marzuq
EGYPT
Aswan
Lake Nasser
SAHARA DESERT
1
Wadi-Halfa
3
Nubian Desert
Port Sudan
NIGER
CHAD
Atbara
Kassala
ERITREA
Khartoum
Asmera
NIGERIA
Lake Chad
Ndjamena
El Fasher
El Obeid
Wad Medani
Lake Tana
DJIBOUTI
Djibouti
Berbera
Kaduna
Abuja
Ibadan
SUDAN
Addis Ababa
SOMALIA
Benue
CENTRAL AFRICAN REPUBLIC
Blue Nile
ETHIOPIA
CAMEROON
Bangui
Bomu
Malabo
Douala
Yaoundé
EQUATORIAL GUINEA
Libreville
SAO TOME & PRINCIPE
GABON
CONGO
Mbandaka
ZAIRE
Kisangani
Congo
UGANDA
Kampala
Lake Victoria
KENYA
Kisumu
Nairobi
Tana
Mogadishu
Kismayu
RWANDA
Bukavu
Kigali
Bujumbura
BURUNDI
Mwanza
Mt Kilimanjaro
4
Mombasa
Dodoma
Zanzibar
Dar-es-Salaam
Brazzaville
Kinshasa
Kananga
Lake Tanganyika
Rufiji
TANZANIA
Luanda
Likasi
Lubumbashi
Lake Nyasa
Moroni
COMOROS
Antsiranana
ANGOLA
Lobito
Huambo
Ndola
MALAWI
Lilongwe
Moçambique
Mahajanga
Namibe
Oubangui
ZAMBIA
Lusaka
Blantyre
MADAGASCAR
Zambezi
Victoria Falls
2
Harare
MOZAMBIQUE
Beira
Antananarivo
NAMIBIA
Windhoek
Okavango Delta
ZIMBABWE
Bulawayo
Limpopo
Fianarantsoa
Namib Desert
BOTSWANA
Kalahari Desert
Gaborone
Pretoria (Tshwane)
Mbabane
Maputo
SWAZILAND
Johannesburg
Bloemfontein
Maseru
LESOTHO
Durban
SOUTH AFRICA
Orange
Great Karoo
DRAKENSBERG
East London
6
Cape Town
7
Cape of Good Hope

AFRICA

People, places, plants and animals

Africa is changing as more people move into cities, where 30% of Africans now live. The biggest cities include Cairo (Egypt) and Lagos (Nigeria). The Sahara and other deserts have hardly any people. Wildlife is under threat, but protected in game reserves.

THE PEOPLE OF AFRICA

In the north of Africa, most people are Arabs and Berbers. In the south, most people are black Africans, with some people of European and Asian origin. More than 800 languages are spoken, but many people speak English, French, Spanish or Portuguese. Africa's two main religions are Christianity and Islam.

The baobab is an African tree with a very thick trunk. Baobabs can live for a thousand years. People make paper and cloth from the bark, and the fruit can be eaten or made into a cooling drink.

Lions are probably Africa's best-known animals. Male lions lead a pride, or group, of female lionesses and cubs.

6 **African culture** is rich and varied, and includes music and dance, sculpture, metalwork and storytelling. The Zulus of South Africa have a proud history, and traditional dancers perform impressively with ox hide shields and short spears.

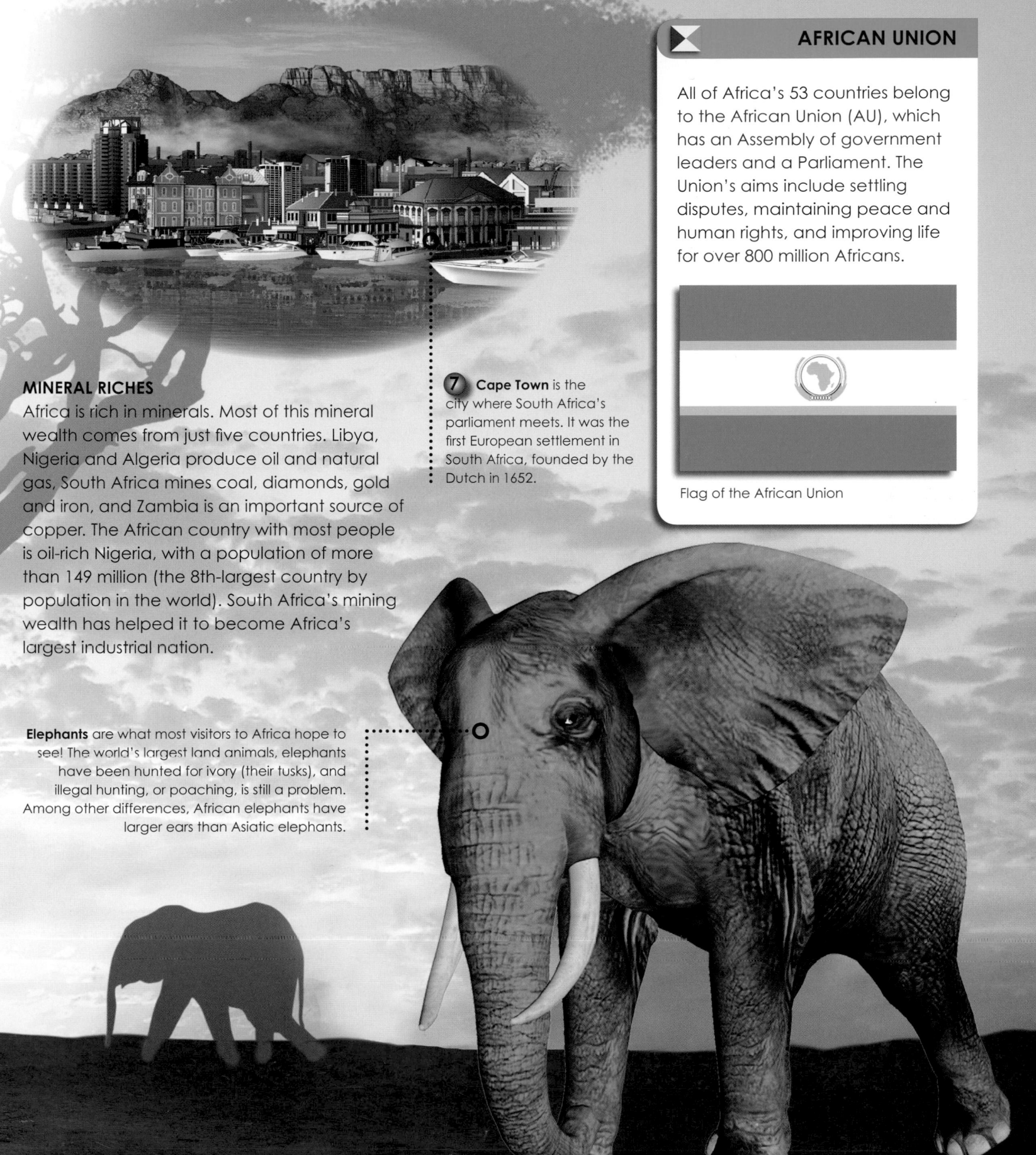

AFRICAN UNION

All of Africa's 53 countries belong to the African Union (AU), which has an Assembly of government leaders and a Parliament. The Union's aims include settling disputes, maintaining peace and human rights, and improving life for over 800 million Africans.

Flag of the African Union

MINERAL RICHES

Africa is rich in minerals. Most of this mineral wealth comes from just five countries. Libya, Nigeria and Algeria produce oil and natural gas, South Africa mines coal, diamonds, gold and iron, and Zambia is an important source of copper. The African country with most people is oil-rich Nigeria, with a population of more than 149 million (the 8th-largest country by population in the world). South Africa's mining wealth has helped it to become Africa's largest industrial nation.

7 **Cape Town** is the city where South Africa's parliament meets. It was the first European settlement in South Africa, founded by the Dutch in 1652.

Elephants are what most visitors to Africa hope to see! The world's largest land animals, elephants have been hunted for ivory (their tusks), and illegal hunting, or poaching, is still a problem. Among other differences, African elephants have larger ears than Asiatic elephants.

NORTHERN AND WESTERN EUROPE

Climate and landscape

Northern Europe extends from mountainous Scandinavia in the north to the Alps (western Europe's biggest mountains) in the south. These form a natural boundary between northern and southern Europe. In between are low-lying hills and plains that make excellent farmland.

NUMBER OF COUNTRIES
20.

HIGHEST MOUNTAIN
Mont Blanc, on the French/Italian/Swiss border, 15,771ft (4,807m).

LONGEST RIVER
The Rhine, flows north for 865mi (1,390km) from east-central Switzerland to the North Sea.

OUTSTANDING SIGHTS

Stonehenge, a Bronze Age stone circle in Britain.
Historic cities such as Paris, London, Copenhagen, Antwerp and Vienna.
The great castles of Britain, France and Germany.
The fjords of Scandinavia.

The region of northern and western Europe has a very long coastline, and many of the region's countries have historic links to the sea and sea trade. The peninsula of Scandinavia has many long, thin inlets of the sea, called fiords, which were made by glaciers. From these, the Vikings (AD 700s–1000s) set off on epic sea journeys to the large islands in the west, including Iceland, Ireland and Britain. The region's major rivers (once important trade routes) are the Rhine, the Loire and the Danube.

1 **The Matterhorn** lies on the border between Switzerland and Italy in the Alps. Many climbers have risked their lives trying to scale its great height. It soars to 14,692ft (4,478m).

The Northern Lights, or Aurora Borealis, make the sky glow with swirling patterns of light. The brilliant display happens as the solar wind (radiation from the Sun) hits the Earth's atmosphere. It is most often seen in the far north, in the parts of Norway and Sweden that lie within the Arctic Circle.

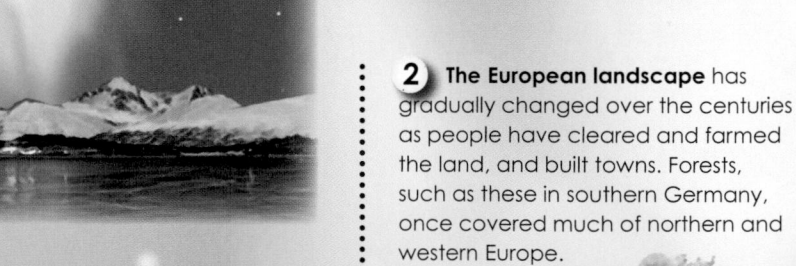

2 **The European landscape** has gradually changed over the centuries as people have cleared and farmed the land, and built towns. Forests, such as these in southern Germany, once covered much of northern and western Europe.

ARCTIC OCEAN

ARCTIC TO MEDITERRANEAN
Iceland and Norway are close to the bitterly cold Arctic Ocean, and so have cold climates. France, by contrast, has a southern coastline on the warm Mediterranean Sea. Winters in Ireland and the United Kingdom are warmed by a North Atlantic warm water current, called the Gulf Stream, while Scandinavia and Germany have much colder winters and more snow.

Reykjavik
ICELAND

Miles
0 — 1000
0 — 1000
Kilometres

The Scottish Highlands have Britain's highest mountains. In the south of Scotland are fertile lowlands and industrial regions.

In Norway, less than 3% of the land is suitable for farming.

Faeroes (DENMARK)

Shetland Islands

NORWEGIAN SEA

SWEDEN

Gulf of Bothnia

FINLAND

Orkney Islands

Hebrides

NORTH SEA

NORWAY

Helsinki

Oslo

Stockholm

Gulf of Finland

Tallinn

SCOTLAND

ESTONIA

Edinburgh

Europe's most spectacular mountains are the Alps. Skiing and other winter sports draw millions of tourists to the Alpine resorts.

Göteborg

LATVIA

NORTHERN IRELAND

Belfast

IRELAND

Dublin

UNITED KINGDOM

DENMARK

Copenhagen

BALTIC SEA

Riga

LITHUANIA

Vilnius

WALES

Cardiff

ENGLAND

Thames

London ③

NETHERLANDS

Hamburg

Elbe

Denmark's flat plains are ideal for farming. Danish farms produce butter, cheese, eggs and bacon.

Scandinavia's mountains are rugged, but not particularly high. The highest peak is Galdhøpiggen in Norway, at 8,100ft (2,469m).

ATLANTIC OCEAN

English Channel

Amsterdam
The Hague

Antwerp

Brussels

BELGIUM

LUXEMBOURG
Luxembourg

Berlin

Oder

GERMANY

Rhine

Seine

Paris ④

Bay of Biscay

Loire

FRANCE

Rhône

②

Danube

Munich

Vienna

AUSTRIA

Limestone caves in southwest France contain cave paintings made by Stone Age people more than 15,000 years ago.

Garonne

MASSIF CENTRAL

Bern

SWITZERLAND

ALPS

①

Mont Blanc ▲

LIECHTENSTEIN

DID YOU KNOW?
The Matterhorn was first climbed in 1865 by British mountaineer Edward Whymper's team. It has four sheer faces, all of which have been climbed.

Lyon

PYRENEES

Monaco

Marseille

Corsica (FRANCE)

MEDITERRANEAN SEA

NORTHERN AND WESTERN EUROPE

People, places, plants and animals

Northern and western Europe are densely populated areas – most people live and work in the cities. Only patches of original wild forest remain. Deciduous trees, such as oak, beech and elm, once covered the warmer parts of the region.

HISTORY AND HERITAGE

Trade and exploring by sea have played an important part in this region's history. The Vikings settled in Britain and Normandy in northern France, and in modern times, migrants have come from eastern Europe, Africa, the Caribbean and Asia. People here speak many languages, and local customs are often preserved in folk festivals. Christianity has left a rich legacy of architecture, from small village churches to magnificent cathedrals. Most countries of northern and western Europe are members of the European Union, and many share the same currency, the Euro. Britain is divided on Europe, and so far has retained its own currency (the pound) and imperial measures, such as miles and pints.

SCANDINAVIA

Rounding up reindeer is a seasonal task for some of the Sámi people of northern Norway, Sweden and Finland – their homeland for more than 2,500 years. A minority of the Sámi are still nomads. They follow their huge reindeer herds to their summer and winter pastures, and use the animals for food, clothing and transportation.

Big Ben is the name of the bell that chimes the hours in the clock tower of the Houses of Parliament in London. The clock tower is often referred to as Big Ben as well. The clock dates from 1859.

DID YOU KNOW?

The world's oldest parliament is the Althing, Iceland's parliament. It was set up by Viking settlers in AD 930.

 **③ The Palace of Westminster,** in London, is where the UK parliament meets. The government is led by the Prime Minister, but the head of state is the queen, Queen Elizabeth II. The United Kingdom is made up of Great Britain (England, Scotland and Wales) and Northern Ireland.

The Eiffel Tower is one of Europe's most famous landmarks. It was built in 1889 for the Universal Exhibition, in celebration of the French Revolution. When it was built, it was the highest structure in the world (184ft/300m).

Europe's forests are home to wild boar (shown here), elk and red deer. These animals have increased in numbers since their natural predators – wolves and lynxes – no longer roam wild, and survive only in national parks. Wild boar are the ancestors of all domestic pigs.

FARMS AND CITIES

Farming was the main occupation in northern and western Europe before 1800 and the Industrial Revolution. Today, far fewer people in the region work on farms. Europe's farms produce cereals, fruit and vegetables, and raise livestock, such as chickens, pigs and cattle. Most farms are large and intensive, although small, family-run farms do still exist, especially in places such as rural France.

The tower is made of 18,038 pieces of iron and steel, held together by 2.5 million rivets. Some 1,665 steps wind their way up to the top of the structure.

French engineer Gustave Eiffel (1832–1923) designed not only the Eiffel Tower, but also the metal framework of the Statue of Liberty in the United States.

DID YOU KNOW?

The Baltic states – Estonia, Latvia and Lithuania – border the Baltic Sea. They broke away from the old Soviet Union in 1990–91. Between them they have only 7 million people.

④ **Paris**, the capital of France, is one of Europe's most historic cities, home of The Louvre Museum and many fine art galleries and restaurants.

The countries of southern and eastern Europe are small and medium-sized. The largest countries in the region are Spain, which takes up most of the Iberian peninsula and, farther east, Poland, Ukraine and Belarus. (In this Atlas, Russia and Turkey, which straddle Europe and Asia, are covered in the Asia region.)

NUMBER OF COUNTRIES
25

HIGHEST MOUNTAIN
Mulhacén, Spain, 11,421ft (3,481m).
Note: Pico de Teide, on the Spanish island of Tenerife, is higher at 12,198ft (3,718m), but Tenerife is geographically part of Africa).

LONGEST RIVER
River Danube, flows eastwards for about 1,770mi (2,850km) from Germany to the Black Sea.

OUTSTANDING SIGHTS

The Parthenon, Athens, Greece – an ancient Greek temple.
The Alcazar, Seville, Spain – a royal palace, originally a Moorish fort.
The Leaning Tower of Pisa, Pisa, Italy.
St Peter's Basilica, Vatican City, Rome, Italy – Europe's biggest church.
Venice, Italy – widely regarded as one of the world's most beautiful cities.

SOUTHERN AND EASTERN EUROPE

Climate and landscape

Many of the countries in this region, such as Spain, Italy, Croatia and Greece, have coasts on the Mediterranean Sea. They have hot, dry summers and warm, wet winters. The inland countries of eastern Europe also have hot summers, but their winters are usually freezing.

VAST, FLAT PLAIN
A vast, flat grassy plain stretches from Poland, in the northwest of the region, south and east through Hungary and Ukraine. These European plains have few trees, but large expanses of grassland and farms producing wheat and other cereals.

1 **The Arbayún Gorge** is a spectacular canyon in the Pyrenees mountains of Spain. In this unspoilt and wild nature reserve, animals such as eagles, vultures, lynxes and bears roam freely.

DID YOU KNOW?

Spain was once several kingdoms. Moors from North Africa invaded in 711 and controlled southern Spain until the 1400s. In 1479 Isabella of Castile married Ferdinand of Aragon, uniting Spain.

Map labels: Porto, Duero, PORTUGAL, Tajo (Tagus), Madrid, Lisbon, Guadiana, SPAIN, Guadalquivir, Seville, Valencia, Malaga, Strait of Gibraltar, Gibraltar (UK), PYRENEES, ANDORRA, Barcelona, MEDITERRANEAN SEA, Palma, BALEARIC IS.

2 **The Dolomites** in northeastern Italy are part of the Alps Mountains. At roughly 9,850ft (3,000m) high, the mountains are popular with skiers in winter, and in summer walkers and campers follow long-distance footpaths.

N

Miles
0 1000
Kilometres
0 1000

DID YOU KNOW?
Europe's smallest state is Vatican City, in Rome, Italy. It is the headquarters of the Roman Catholic Church.

3 The Postojna Caves, with their impressive stalactites and stalagmites, are a tourist attraction in Slovenia. The caves are so big that people can ride inside them on a special train, and one cavern is big enough to be used for orchestral concerts.

BALTIC SEA

Minsk

BELARUS
Pripyat

Warsaw

POLAND

Kiev

6 Prague

CZECH REPUBLIC

SLOVAKIA

UKRAINE

Dnestr

Desna

Dnepr

Bratislava

MOLDOVA
Kishinev
Odessa

Budapest

Prut

ALPS

2

SLOVENIA
3 Ljubljana
Zagreb

Milan
Po
Venice

HUNGARY

CARPATHIANS

ROMANIA

Sevastopol

BLACK SEA

CROATIA

SAN MARINO

Pisa

BOSNIA-
HERZEGOVINA

Belgrade

Bucharest

Danube

4 The Mediterranean Sea has been a trade route for people in ships for thousands of years. The mountainous island of Crete, shown here, was once the home of the rich Minoan civilization. Today it is part of Greece.

ITALY

Tiber

Sarajevo

SERBIA

BULGARIA

Rome
Italy is rich in history, art and architecture. It has many beautiful old towns and priceless paintings and statues.

ADRIATIC SEA

MONTENEGRO
Podgorica

Sofiya

Pristina

KOSOVO

SARDINIA

Naples

Skopje

Cagliari

ALBANIA

Tirane

MACEDONIA

Palermo
SICILY

GREECE

AEGEAN SEA

Athens **5**

Sicily, off the 'toe' of Italy, is one of several large islands in the Mediterranean Sea.

Valletta
MALTA

Greece is famous for ancient temples, olive groves, its many beautiful sunny islands, and for being the birthplace of the Olympic Games.

CRETE **4**

MEDITERRANEAN SEA

Nicosia

CYPRUS

SOUTHERN AND EASTERN EUROPE

People, places, plants and animals

Along the Mediterranean coastline, semi-tropical trees and flowers flourish in the mild, sunny climate, while across much of eastern Europe there are forests and grasslands. Wildlife includes wolves, lynxes, brown bears and wild goats, and many species of birds and insects. Reptiles, such as lizards and tortoises, bask in the sun.

PEOPLES OF THE REGION

Many of the peoples of southern and eastern Europe speak related languages, but there are some oddities. The Basques of Spain, for example, speak Euskara – a language unlike any other. National rivalries in the past were very strong. The Balkans (a region extending from Slovenia across to Romania and south to Greece), for instance, has seen many wars. Most southern and eastern Europeans are Christians, and Roman Catholicism is strong in Spain, Portugal, Italy and Poland. In Greece and Russia, many people belong to the Orthodox churches. The region's population includes many Muslim and Hindu immigrants from Africa and Asia, as well as people of other faiths.

Flamenco accessories include an ornamental hair comb and flowers, and big earrings.

Flamenco is a traditional dance from Spain, originally danced by gypsies or Romanies (people who travel rather than having a fixed home). Flamenco dancers perform to the rhythm of handclaps and the clicking of castanets.

Folk cultures in Europe no longer have such close links to local customs as they once had. Most, such as flamenco dancing, are carried on by enthusiasts or by professionals who perform to entertain tourists.

DID YOU KNOW?

Malta is an island in the Mediterranean. The people speak Maltese, a language with Arabic and Italian roots. Because of its key position as a port, it has been fought over many times in history.

A typical dress has ruffles on the skirt and sleeves.

A huge gateway, called The Propylaea, guards the way up the Acropolis – the hill where the city's treasury was located.

5 In Athens, the ancient Greeks experimented with democracy over 2,000 years ago. Ancient Greece is called 'the cradle of Western civilization.'

The dancer makes a rhythmic combination of sounds by stepping with the toe, sole and heel of the foot.

IBEX

The ibex is a wild goat found in the mountains of southern Europe, and also in north Africa and parts of Asia. It is an agile climber, scrambling over steep rocks with ease. Ibexes have long, curving horns. They live in small herds, each led by a male.

6 Prague's famous astronomical clock dates from the 1400s. It has a 24-hour dial, and also shows the time of sunrise and sunset, among other things. Prague is the capital of the Czech Republic (formerly Bohemia).

FARMING AND INDUSTRY

The richest industrial countries in this region include Spain, Italy, Poland, the Czech Republic and Hungary. Most of the region's countries are members of the European Union, and all trade with one another by sea and across land borders. There are many small farms, where families grow crops such as wheat, grapes, olives, fruit and vegetables. Tourism is important, especially in the Mediterranean, where old fishing villages have become popular holiday resorts.

The Parthenon is one of the world's greatest cultural monuments. This ancient Greek temple was built (447 to 438 BC) on the Acropolis, overlooking Athens. It was dedicated to the goddess Athena.

Although now a ruin, the Parthenon is visited by thousands of tourists each year. It was originally decorated with a frieze of sculptures (now in museums in London and Athens) of the gods and heroes of ancient Greece. Inside was a huge statue of the goddess Athena, covered in ivory and gold. It stood about 40ft (12m) high.

46 columns surround the Parthenon.

RUSSIA, WEST AND SOUTH ASIA

Climate and landscape

In such a huge area there are vast differences in climate and landscape, from the cold treeless tundra of the far north to the lush tropical forests of the south, and the dry deserts of Arabia and Iraq in the west.

CLIMATE EXTREMES

Siberia and Central Asia can be extremely cold, with winter temperatures of 3.2°F (-16°C). In contrast, Arabian heat can exceed 113°F (45°C). In the Indian sub-continent, the monsoon's seasonal winds bring heavy rain to end the dry season.

Asia is the world's largest continent, and western Asia forms the greater part of it. It includes the vast expanse of Siberia in Russia, the huge Indian sub-continent, the deserts of Arabia and the countries around the Caspian Sea, Persian Gulf and eastern Mediterranean.

NUMBER OF COUNTRIES
31

HIGHEST MOUNTAIN
Mount Everest, between Nepal and China, is 29,035ft (8,850m) in height (as recalculated in the 1990s).

LONGEST RIVER
The River Lena, in Russia, is 2,734mi (4,400km). (The Yenisei River, at 3,445mi (5,539 km) is longer, but starts outside this region in Mongolia.)

OUTSTANDING SIGHTS

The Dead Sea, bordering Israel, the West Bank and Jordan – the world's lowest and saltiest sea.
The Ka'aba in Mecca, Saudi Arabia – a building within a mosque, where Muslim pilgrims gather.
The Taj Mahal, India – a magnificent marble tomb built for a Mughal princess.
The Kremlin, Russia – the heart of power in Moscow.
Jerusalem, Israel – a city sacred to Christianity, Islam and Judaism.
The Basilica Cistern in Istanbul, Turkey.

DIVERSE LANDSCAPES

Vast stretches of the north of this region are mountainous or covered in inhospitable tundra or forest that extends for thousands of miles. In the west, much of the region is desert. The most populated part of western Asia is India, where the climate and landscape are better suited to farming, and seasonal rainfall is usually reliable. However, droughts and floods do also occur here.

1 **Mount Everest**, in the Himalayas, is the world's highest mountain. Its mighty peak was first climbed in 1953 by New Zealander Edmund Hillary and Tenzing Norgay from Nepal.

The Russian taiga (or boreal forest) is a belt of mainly coniferous forest that extends in a broad band across the north of the region. Here, spruce, fir, pine and birch trees survive the long winters and short summers.

Mediterranean Sea
ARMENIA
GEORGIA
AZERBA
Istanbul
Black Sea
2
Ankara
CAUCAS
TURKEY
LEBANON
ISRAEL
Jerusalem
Damascus
SYRIA
Amman
JORDAN
Euphrates
Tigris
Casp Se
Baghdad
IRAQ
Tehran
SAUDI ARABIA
Kuwait
IRA
KUWAIT
ZAGROS MTS.
Medina
BAHRAIN
Al Manamah
Red Sea
Mecca
Riyadh
Doha
The Gulf
QATAR
Abu Dhabi
UNITED ARAB EMIRATES
Muscat
Sana
YEMEN
OMAN
Gulf of Aden

ARCTIC OCEAN

The tundra is a treeless region that extends across the far north. It is freezing and snow-covered in winter.

Bering Sea

The Kamchatka Peninsula at the eastern tip of Russia has active volcanoes, geysers and hot springs.

Murmansk

Novaya Zemlya

Kara Sea

Laptev Sea

St Petersburg

Nordvik

CENTRAL SIBERIAN PLATEAU

Kolyma

Indigirka

Moscow

Pechora

Ob'

Yenisey

Lena

URAL MOUNTAINS

Volga

Kazan

Siberian Lowland

Nizhnyaya Tunguska

RUSSIA

Sea of Okhotsk

Yekaterinburg

Ob'

Volgograd

Ural

Tobol

Yenisey

Lensk

Angara

Omsk

Novosibirsk

Ishim

Ir-tysh

KAZAKHSTAN

Lena

Amur

Astana

Aral Sea

Syr Darya

Lake Baykal

SAYAN MTS.

Irkutsk

Khabarovsk

UZBEKISTAN

Lake Balkhash

Lake Baikal is the world's deepest lake. Over 390mi (630km) long, the lake is 5,315ft (1,620m) deep at its deepest point.

PACIFIC OCEAN

MENISTAN

shkhabad

Amu Darya

Tashkent

Bishkek

KYRGYZSTAN

Dushanbe

The Himalayas are the world's highest mountains, with 14 peaks over 26,200ft (8,000m) high. Other mighty Central Asian mountain ranges are the Pamirs, Karakorum and Hindu Kush.

Vladivostok

GHANISTAN

TAJIKISTAN

Kabul

HINDU KUSH

Islamabad *(disputed area)*

DID YOU KNOW?

Lake Baikal contains more fresh water than any other lake in the world. It is home to the freshwater Baikal seal.

PAKISTAN

Lahore

Indus

HIMALAYAS

Karachi

Delhi

NEPAL

3

Kathmandu

1

Mt. Everest

N

INDIA

Ganges

BHUTAN

Thimphu

BANGLADESH

Mumbai (Bombay)

Kolkata (Calcutta)

Dhaka

Hyderabad

| 0 | Miles | 1000 |
| 0 | Kilometres | 1000 |

Bay of Bengal

2 **In Turkey**, a country that 'bridges' Asia to Europe, unusual hot springs at Pamukkale form terraces of snowlike chalk deposits. Visitors have come to marvel at them since ancient Greek and Roman times.

Chennai (Madras)

SRI LANKA

Colombo

INDIAN OCEAN

RUSSIA, WEST AND SOUTH ASIA
People, places, plants and animals

Western Asia has an amazing variety of people. In Siberia, in the cold north, small bands of nomads wander with herds of reindeer, while in the warm south India's cities teem with millions of people. The region's wildlife has adapted to grassy plains, dense cold forests, tropical jungles, swamps and deserts.

BIRTHPLACE OF ANCIENT CULTURES

Asia was the birthplace of the world's great religions: Hinduism, Judaism, Buddhism, Christianity and Islam. Russia is mainly Christian, India mostly Hindu. The most widespread religion across western Asia is Islam. The region was also home to some of history's greatest civilizations, such as those of Mesopotamia (Iraq), Persia (Iran) and the Indus Valley and Mughal eras (India).

MANY CUSTOMS, MANY LANGUAGES

The people of Western Asia speak many languages. There are hundreds of local languages, for example, in India alone, which has more than one billion people and is the world's second-largest country by population. Religion can be a unifying force. Across the Muslim world, from Arabia to Pakistan, family life for many people is governed by religious laws.

3 **The Taj Mahal in Agra, India,** is widely thought of as one of the most beautiful buildings in the world. It was built by the Mughal emperor Shah Jahan as a tomb for his wife, Mumtaz Mahal, after she died in 1631.

RUSSIA

St Basil's Cathedral in Moscow, Russia, is a magnificent Christian church. Eight chapels surround the tall, central structure, each with a distinctive, brightly painted onion-shaped dome. The cathedral was built by the Russian Tsar Ivan IV ('the Terrible') from 1555 to 1561.

DID YOU KNOW?

Across western Asia, closely related animals have adapted to very different environments. Siberian tigers live in snowy forests, while Indian tigers hunt in hot swamps and jungles.

The water garden, with its many fountains, is fed by a system of underground pipes and pumps from the River Yamuna.

The Bactrian camel is one of two species of camel found in Western Asia. It is shaggy-haired, with two humps. Bactrian camels live across Central Asia and withstand cold better than the one-humped camel of Arabia.

DID YOU KNOW?

Saudi Arabia has about one fourth of the world's oil reserves, and the world's biggest airport, at Riyadh. In the south, the Rub Al-Khali (Empty Quarter) is the world's largest sand desert.

ADAPTING TO THE DESERT

In the deserts of Western Asia, drinking water is found only at waterholes, or oases. Desert animals are adapted to live on very little water and food. A camel can go for days without water, using the moisture in the plants it eats. It stores fat in its hump. On its feet are pads to help it walk over soft sand. Many smaller desert animals, such as sand cats, jerboas and scorpions, come out at night, when it is cool, and seek shelter in burrows or beneath rocks during the heat of the day. Many kinds of plants have adapted to the desert, too. They either need very little water to survive, or are salt tolerant.

Money from oil has changed the lives of many people. The rulers of Saudi Arabia and the Gulf states, such as Kuwait, have used money from oil to build palaces, cities, roads, schools, hospitals and hotels on land that a hundred years ago was empty desert.

Oil wells in Arabia, Iraq and the Gulf states are a sign of this region's oil-wealth. Some states are tiny, but immensely rich.

EAST AND SOUTHEAST ASIA

Climate and landscape

From high mountains in the north and southwest flow some of the region's major rivers, such as the Huang He, Yangtze, Salween, Irrawaddy and Mekong. In the south, the climate is hot with dry and rainy seasons. In the north, winters are cold and summers hot, often with little rain. Beyond the barren Gobi Desert lie the steppes or grassy plains of Mongolia. To the east are a number of large island groups, including Japan, the Philippines and Indonesia.

East and Southeast Asia includes China, the world's third-largest country by area and the largest by population. This region is one of the most densely populated on the planet, with huge, crowded cities especially in Japan and parts of Indonesia.

NUMBER OF COUNTRIES
16

HIGHEST MOUNTAIN
Aksai Chin 1 (The Kunlun Goddess) is 23,514ft, (7,167m) high.
For Mount Everest, shared by Nepal and China, see Western Asia.

LONGEST RIVER
The Yangtze River, China, is 3,915mi (6,300km) long.

OUTSTANDING SIGHTS

The Great Wall of China – the longest structure built by humans.
Hong Kong, China – an island of skyscrapers.
The Petronas Towers, Kuala Lumpur, Malaysia – one of the world's tallest buildings.
The Temple of Angkor Wat, Cambodia – a Hindu temple from the 1100s.
The forests of Borneo – home to orang-utans.
Tokyo, Japan – with its busy Ginza shopping district.
The Forbidden City, Beijing – once the home of China's emperors.
Mayon, the Philippines – a cone-shaped volcano.

1 **Mount Fuji** is Japan's highest mountain, at 12,388ft (3,776m). Like many mountains in this region, Fuji is a volcano. It is a sacred place to many Japanese people.

2 Cambodia is one of the countries where severe flooding is frequently a problem, so boats become the best means of transport. Many people in Southeast Asia live beside or on the water, in houseboats or in houses built on stilts.

WEATHER EFFECTS
Monsoon winds blow from inland across Southeast Asia between November and March, bringing drier, cooler weather. From May to October, the winds blow from the opposite direction, from over the Indian Ocean, and bring heavy rain – sometimes so heavy it causes severe flooding.

The islands of the Pacific rim, such as Japan, are geologically active. Volcanic eruptions and earthquakes are frequent, and can cause massive damage.

The Turfan Depression in northwest China is a vast basin surrounded by mountains. It is 508ft (155m) below sea level.

When the Indonesian volcano Krakatoa blew its top in 1883, the noise was heard 3,000mi (4,800km) away.

Rice is the single most important food in much of Asia. Rice plants are planted in flooded paddy fields, which are drained dry before the crop is harvested.

Borneo is the world's third-largest island. The island is divided between Malaysia, Indonesia and the tiny oil-rich state of Brunei.

(3) **Spectacular cone-shaped limestone hills** surround the city of Guilin in southern China. This beautiful scenery has long been an inspiration to China's artists.

Map labels: TIAN SHAN, MONGOLIA, Ulan Bator, Manchurian Plain, Harbin, Sapporo, Gobi Desert, Changchun, Shenyang, NORTH KOREA, JAPAN, Sea of Japan, KUNLUN SHAN, Beijing, Pyongyang, Seoul, SOUTH KOREA, Tokyo, Osaka, PLATEAU OF TIBET, CHINA, Xi'an, Great Basin, Yellow Sea, Huang He, HIMALAYAS, Mt. Everest, Yangtze (Chang Jiang), Wuhan, Shanghai, East China Sea, PACIFIC OCEAN, Irrawaddy, Guangzhou, Hong Kong, MYANMAR, Hanoi, LAOS, South China Sea, Naypyidaw, Vientiane, Salween, Philippine Sea, Bay of Bengal, Yangon (Rangoon), Hue, Mekong, Da Nang, Luzon, Moulmein, THAILAND, VIETNAM, Manila, Bangkok, CAMBODIA, Phnom Penh, Ho Chi Minh City, PHILIPPINES, Mindanao, INDIAN OCEAN, BRUNEI, Celebes Sea, Kuala Lumpur, MALAYSIA, Bandar Seri Begawan, Singapore, SINGAPORE, Pontianak, Borneo, Celebes, Sumatra, Coral Sea, INDONESIA, Djakarta, Java, Dili

EAST AND SOUTHEAST ASIA
People, places, plants and animals

Many Asian people live near rivers or the sea, where they can fish for a living, or in mountain valleys, where they farm the land. The region also has some of the world's largest cities, such as Tokyo in Japan and Djakarta in Indonesia. Wild places are becoming scarce, and large land animals, such as the Asian rhino and tiger, survive only in small numbers.

DID YOU KNOW?

Indonesia is home to the world's largest lizard, the Komodo dragon. It lives on Komodo Island. A type of monitor lizard, it can grow up to 9.8ft (3m) long, and is big enough to eat a goat.

A RICH MIX OF CULTURES
Many of the goods bought by people in Europe and the USA are made in Asia. China, Japan, South Korea and even tiny Singapore are world leaders in finance and industry. There is a rich mix of cultures, here, too – both ancient and modern. The latest gadgets and computer games are enjoyed alongside traditional forms of music and dance.

FAMILY LIFE
Family life is important in most Asian societies, with extended families often sharing the same home. China, however, has a strict 'one-child' policy, imposed by the government to control the rising population.

4 **There are many giant statues of the Buddha** in Thailand, including this 82ft (25m) high statue in Narathiwat. Buddhists follow the teachings of the Buddha, Siddhartha Gautama (c.563–483 BC), an Indian prince who became dissatisfied with a life of pleasure.

RELIGIONS
The peoples of East and Southeast Asia follow several religions, including Christianity (in the Philippines), Islam (Indonesia), Shinto (Japan) and Buddhism, which is widespread across the region. In China, many people still follow the teachings of Confucius, an ancient Chinese teacher (551– 479 BC), although after China's Communist revolution of 1949 religion was discouraged.

The image of the Buddha is an object of religious devotion and respect to followers of his teachings. Yellow- or orange-robed Buddhist monks are a common sight in Thailand, Myanmar, Laos and Cambodia.

WILDLIFE UNDER THREAT

In much of East and Southeast Asia, millions of people live in busy cities or in intensively farmed countryside. Human pressure squeezes out wild plants and animals into remote forests and mountains. Bamboo grows so fast it is unlikely to die out, but forest trees such as teak and sandalwood are at risk from loggers. Forests have also been cleared to make way for farms and rubber plantations. This affects animals, such as the orang-utan, which suffer from loss of habitat and human interference. Conservationists are working to protect the region's rare animals and unusual plants, such as the world's largest flower, the Rafflesia, which measures up to 39in (1m) across.

NORTHERN PLAINS

The high plains, deserts and mountains of northern China and Mongolia are a contrast to the forests of the south. In this harsh landscape, horses are often a more useful form of transport than trucks. There are few trees, and most people are nomadic herders, wandering with their horses, camels and sheep across the windswept grasslands.

In Mongolia, nomads live in yurts – tentlike dwellings made from felt cloth that can be carried by a pack animal. Many nomads also own a satellite dish, used not only to recieve TV signals, but also to fry eggs on!

5 **Floating markets**, such as this one on the Mekong River in Vietnam, are a common sight along the waterways of Southeast Asia. People sell fresh fruit and vegetables from their boats.

DID YOU KNOW?

The Rafflesia flower smells like rotting meat. The smell attracts insects, which transport pollen from male to female flowers.

AUSTRALASIA

Climate and landscape

Much of Australia is hot and dry, with rainfall plentiful only in the southeast. Most of the interior is flat. New Zealand has a mountainous landscape, more rain and more lush vegetation. Papua New Guinea is hot and humid, with forests and mountains. Most of the Pacific islands are low-lying.

THE OUTBACK

Australia covers about 5% of the Earth's land area. Two thirds of the island-continent is desert. Australians call the interior 'the outback.' Large parts of the outback provide good grazing land for sheep and cattle, which are kept on huge farms or 'stations,' often far from a town.

Australasia is the name for Australia and the areas around it, including New Zealand and Papua New Guinea. Oceania is a region that includes Australasia and the 30,000 or so islands dotted across the vast Pacific Ocean.

NUMBER OF COUNTRIES
14

HIGHEST MOUNTAIN
Mt Wilhelm, Papua New Guinea, at 14,793ft (4,509m) high.

LONGEST RIVER
Murray River, Australia, at 1,572mi (2,530km) long.

OUTSTANDING SIGHTS

Wave rock, Hyden, Western Australia – a huge rock, over 2,700 million years old.
Uluru (also known as Ayers Rock), central Australia – a sacred place for Aboriginals.
The Great Barrier Reef, off the coast of Queensland, northeastern Australia – the biggest coral reef in the world.
Ceremonial dancing, Papua New Guinea.
Maori carvings, New Zealand.
Sydney Harbour Bridge and Opera House, Sydney, Australia.

Miles
0 500

Kilometres
0 500

N

ARAFURA SEA

Melville I.
Bathurst I.
Darwin
Arr...
Daly
Wyndham
C. Lévêque
Kimberley Plateau
Derby
Fitzroy
NORTHERN TERRITORY
Port Hedland
Great Sandy Desert
North West C.
Fortescue
Mt. Bruce
MACDON...
Gibson Desert
Uluru (Ayers...
Carnarvon
WESTERN AUSTRALIA
Murchison
Great Victoria Desert
Geraldton
Nullarbor Plain
① Kalgoorlie-Boulder
Perth
Fremantle
Great Australian Bight
C. Leeuwin
Albany

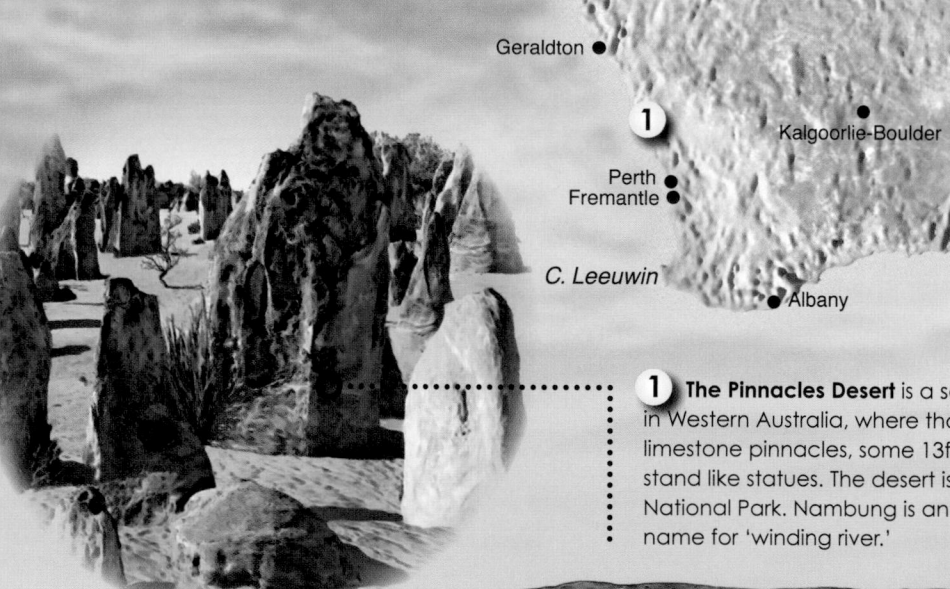

① The Pinnacles Desert is a sandy region in Western Australia, where thousands of limestone pinnacles, some 13ft (4m) high, stand like statues. The desert is in Nambung National Park. Nambung is an Aboriginal name for 'winding river.'

PACIFIC OCEAN

Bismarck Archipelago
New Ireland
BISMARCK SEA
New Britain
PAPUA NEW GUINEA
SOLOMON SEA
Gulf of Papua
Torres Strait
C. York
Port Moresby
Gulf of Carpentaria
Groote Eylandt

Bougainville I.
SOLOMON ISLANDS
Choiseul
Santa Isabel
Honiara
Malaita
Guadalcanal
San Cristobal

The Pacific islands are divided into three main groups: Melanesia, Micronesia and Polynesia. The islands are warm and sunny, though tropical storms called typhoons may rush in from the ocean. Coconut palms and luxuriant flowers flourish on the islands.

Espiritu Santo
Malakula
VANUATU
Port-Vila
Vanua Levu
FIJI
Suva
Viti Levu

DID YOU KNOW?

When you think of Australia, you may think of surfing and sandy beaches. But you can ski there, too, in the Snowy Mountains.

CORAL SEA

GREAT DIVIDING RANGE
Cairns
Mitchell
Flinders
Townsville

Rockhampton
Diamantina
Thomson
Barcoo
QUEENSLAND
Fraser I.
Brisbane

Simpson Desert
L. Eyre
ALIA
L. Torrens
Darling
NEW SOUTH WALES
GREAT DIVIDING RANGE
Lachlan
Newcastle
④ Sydney
Wollongong
Elizabeth
Adelaide
Murray
Canberra
VICTORIA
Mt. Kosciusko
AUSTRALIAN CAPITAL TERRITORY
Kangaroo I.
Ballarat
Melbourne
C. Howe
Geelong
King I.
Bass Strait
Flinders I.
SOUTHERN OCEAN
TASMANIA
Launceston
Hobart

③ **The Great Barrier Reef** stretches for more than 1,300mi (2,100km) along the eastern coast of Australia. It is a living structure, made by tiny sea creatures called coral polyps. These attach themselves to the rocks in great numbers. The reef is also home to 1,500 kinds of fish, as well as turtles, crabs, starfish and sponges.

NEW ZEALAND

Much of New Zealand is covered in open grassland, ideal for sheep farming. About a quarter of the land is tree-covered.

② **Uluru**, meaning 'great pebble,' is a massive sandstone rock that rises 1,142ft (348m) out of the desert in the Northern Territory of Australia.

Auckland
NORTH ISLAND
L. Taupo
NEW ZEALAND
Ruapehu
Wellington
SOUTHERN ALPS
SOUTH ISLAND
Christchurch
Stewart I.

New Zealand's highest mountains are the Southern Alps in South Island. There are also hot springs, fast-flowing rivers and glaciers. The climate is mild with good rainfall.

AUSTRALASIA

People, places, plants and animals

Australia and New Zealand were among the last lands to be settled by Europeans. The Aboriginal peoples of Australia probably came from Asia many thousands of years ago, and the Maoris of New Zealand sailed to their new home from Polynesia more than 1,000 years ago. Australasia's animals and plants include species not found anywhere else.

FARMING AND MINERAL WEALTH

Australia and New Zealand are famous for sheep farms. Farmers also raise dairy and beef cattle, and grow wheat, rice, fruit and vegetables. New Zealand gets electricity from water and geothermal (underground heat) power, but has few minerals. Australia's valuable minerals include uranium, bauxite, diamonds, iron, coal, tin and oil. The much smaller Pacific islands have few industries; most people live by fishing, farming and tourism. Some of the islands do have minerals, however, such as phosphates on Nauru, nickel and other minerals on New Caledonia (a French overseas territory), and gold on Fiji and the Solomon Islands.

④ The Sydney Opera House, completed in 1973, is Australia's best-known landmark, with its white roofs reminding people of a ship's sails. Australia has produced many fine actors, singers and sports stars.

Port Jackson is the huge inlet beside which Sydney is built. The land was home to various groups of Aboriginals before it was discovered by Lt. James Cook in 1770. Cook named the inlet after Sir George Jackson, his friend and patron.

ABORIGINALS

The Aboriginal people's skill at hunting and food-gathering helped them survive in the harsh conditions of the outback. Their hunting weapons included the woomera (a spear-throwing device) and the boomerang. Most Aboriginals now live and work on farms or in towns. They have a rich tradition of dance, storytelling rock painting and engraving.

Natural body paints are worn by Aboriginal dancers.

Kiwi fruit are named after New Zealand's national bird, the Kiwi. The plant comes from China, but New Zealand is the world's leading producer of kiwi fruit.

Passion fruit is another plant that was introduced to Australasia. The passion flower vine is native to South America.

UNIQUE ANIMALS

Australia's unusual animals include species found nowhere else on Earth. There are about 150 kinds of marsupials (mammals that carry their young in pouches), including kangaroos, wallabies, koalas, wombats and bandicoots. Even more remarkable are the platypus and echidna, which are the world's only egg-laying mammals.

FISHING AND TOURISM

The Pacific Ocean is a rich fishing ground, and many people in the region, especially the Pacific islanders, make their living from fishing. Tourism is also an important industry. Visitors to Australia enjoy its beaches and water sports, such as surfing. But swimmers do have to watch out for sharks, because these waters are home to the world's fiercest shark, the great white. Many people travel to New Zealand to hike in the mountains, sail or go whale-watching in the southwestern Pacific Ocean.

Koala

Kangaroo

Sydney Harbour Bridge was opened in 1932. Its steel arch stretches 1,650ft (502m) across the Paramatta River.

Modern Sydney grew on the spot where British settlers landed in 1788. Today, over 80% of Australians live in cities.

ATLANTIC OCEAN

THE POLES

Climate and landscape

The Arctic includes the Arctic Ocean and the northern parts of the continents of Europe, Asia and North America. **The Antarctic** is a landmass hidden under thick ice. Plant fossils show that it was once warm and ice-free.

NUMBER OF COUNTRIES
Countries that have land within the Arctic Circle are Canada, Greenland (Denmark), Norway and Russia.

Seven countries claim territories in the Antarctic.

HIGHEST MOUNTAIN
Mount Vinson, the highest peak of the Vinson Massif in Antarctica, is 16,050ft (4,892m).

LARGEST GLACIER
The Lambert Glacier in Antarctica is the world's biggest glacier. It is more than 37mi (60km) wide.

OUTSTANDING SIGHTS

The North Pole, first reached by American explorer Robert Peary in 1909 (disputed by some experts).
The South Pole, first reached by Norwegian explorer Roald Amundsen in 1911.
Vostok Station, Antarctica, where, in 1983, the coldest-ever temperature, -128.56°F (-89.2°C), was recorded.

The Earth has two polar regions, bitterly cold and mostly snow-covered. The area around the North Pole, the Arctic, consists mostly of the Arctic Ocean, which is frozen for much of the year. The area around the South Pole, the Antarctic, is an icy continent, bigger than the United States, but covered by ice averaging 6,500ft (2,000m) thick.

Claims to parts of Antarctica have been made by seven countries, Argentina, Australia, Chile, Britain, France, New Zealand and Norway, but none of these are recognized internationally.

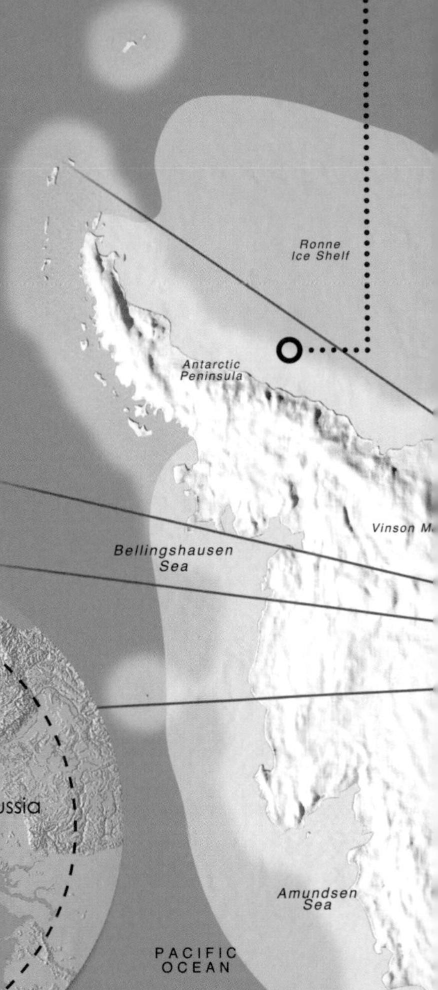

Ronne Ice Shelf

Antarctic Peninsula

Vinson M

Bellingshausen Sea

Amundsen Sea

PACIFIC OCEAN

THE FROZEN ARCTIC OCEAN

The map shows the average extent of the Arctic sea ice, but global warming is causing the ice to melt, especially in summer. The Arctic Circle is roughly 1,615mi (2,600km) from the North Pole.

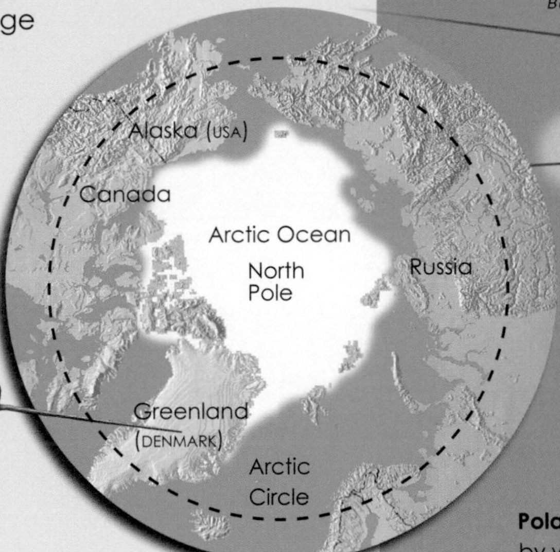

Alaska (USA)

Canada

Arctic Ocean

North Pole

Russia

Greenland (DENMARK)

Arctic Circle

The narwhal is a small Arctic whale. The males are unusual in having a long, corkscrew-like tusk 7–10ft (2–3m) long.

Polar bears hunt seals by walking across the Arctic ice. If global warming melts the ice, the bears will not be able to find food in this way.

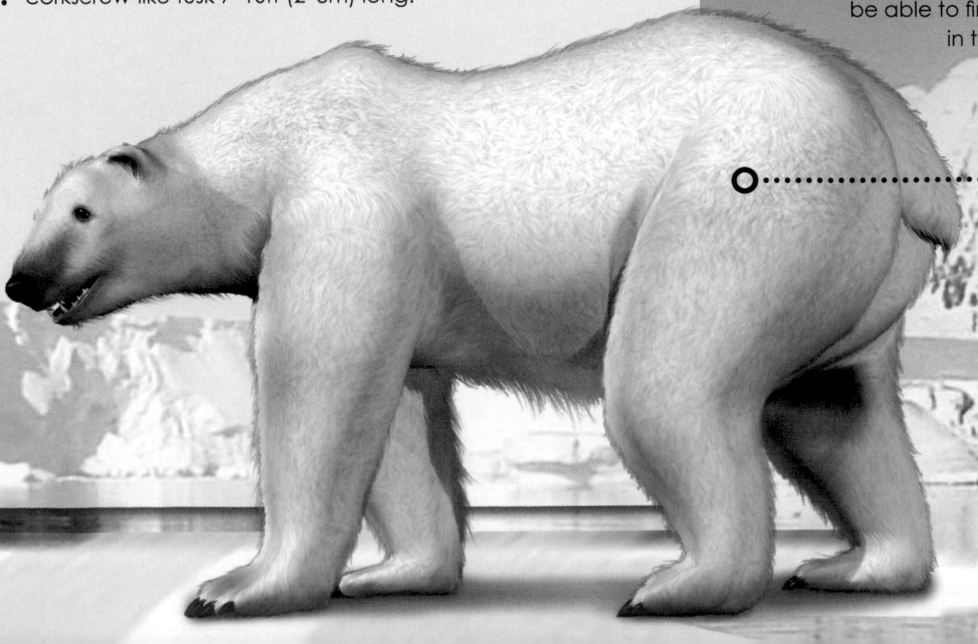

① **The Amundsen-Scott** station is where scientists live and work at the South Pole. It is named for the Antarctic's two most famous explorers Roald Amundsen of Norway and Robert F. Scott of the UK.

INDIAN OCEAN

Dronning Maud Land

Enderby Land

EAST ANTARCTICA

① South Pole

TRANSANTARCTIC MOUNTAINS

WEST ANTARCTICA

Vostok Station

Ross Ice Shelf

Victoria Land

South Magnetic Pole

Mount William is a 4,970ft (1,514m) peak located on Anvers Island near Palmer Station, one of three US research stations.

0   Miles   1000
0   Kilometres   1000

THE FROZEN CONTINENT
Unlike the Arctic, which long ago was settled by Inuit and other nomadic hunters, the Antarctic has no permanent population. However, during the summer scientists work at more than 30 scientific bases, including McMurdo Station, which is big enough for about 1,000 people. There is very little plant or animal life on the frozen continent, but the seas are rich in plankton, krill, fish, birds, seals and whales.

PENGUINS

Emperor penguins live in Antarctic colonies, hunting for fish in the sea. Emperor chicks need plenty of fat and downy feathers to keep out the cold.

Adult Emperor penguin

Penguin chicks

AMAZING FACTS AND FIGURES

Here are some statistics about the most amazing things on Earth.

In 1800, the Earth was home to about 1 billion people. The population passed 5 billion in 1987, and 6 billion in 1999. It is now about 6.7 billion. Most of those billions of people live on less than 20% of the planet.

THE WORLD'S TOP FIVE COUNTRIES BY AREA

1 Russia	6,592,800sq mi	(17,075,400sq km)
2 Canada	3,855,103sq mi	(9,984,670sq km)
3 China	3,696,100sq mi	(9,572,900sq km)
4 USA	3,676,487sq mi	(9,522,058sq km)
5 Brazil	3,287,612sq mi	(8,514,877sq km)

THE WORLD'S TOP 25 COUNTRIES BY POPULATION (2009)

Country	Population
1 China	1,338,613,000
2 India	1,166,079,000
3 United States	307,212,000
4 Indonesia	240,272,000
5 Brazil	198,739,000
6 Pakistan	176,243,000
7 Bangladesh	156,051,000
8 Nigeria	149,229,000
9 Russia	140,041,000
10 Japan	127,079,000
11 Mexico	111,212,000
12 Philippines	97,977,000
13 Vietnam	86,968,000
14 Ethiopia	85,237,000
15 Egypt	83,083,000
16 Germany	82,330,000
17 Turkey	76,806,000
18 Congo (Kinshasa)	68,693,000
19 Iran	66,429,000
20 Thailand	65,905,000
21 France	64,420,000
22 United Kingdom	61,113,000
23 Italy	58,126,000
24 South Africa	49,052,000
25 South Korea	48,509,000

DID YOU KNOW?

The Earth's rocky crust is thickest under the continents and much thinner under the oceans.

THE BIGGEST OCEANS

1 Pacific Ocean	64 million sq mi	(165 million sq km)
2 Atlantic Ocean	32 million sq mi	(82 million sq km)
3 Indian Ocean	28 million sq mi	(73 million sq km)

THE LONGEST RIVERS

1 Nile, Africa	4,132mi	(6,650km)
2 Amazon, South America	4,000mi	(6,400km)
3 Yangtze (Chang Jiang), China	3,915mi	(6,300km)
4 Huang He (Yellow), China	3,395mi	(5,464km)
5 Congo (Zaire), Africa	2,900mi	(4,700km)

THE HIGHEST WATERFALLS

1 Angel, Venezuela	3,212ft	(979m)
2 Tugela, Africa	3,110ft	(948m)
3 Utigord, Norway	2,624ft	(800m)
4 Monge Falls, Norway	2,539ft	(774m)
5 Yosemite, USA	2,425ft	(739m)

THE LARGEST LAKES/INLAND SEAS

1 Caspian Sea, Asia	149,200sq mi (386,400sq km)
2 Lake Superior, North America	31,700sq mi (82,100sq km)
3 Lake Victoria, Africa	26,828sq mi (69,484sq km)
4 Lake Huron, North America	23,000sq mi (59,570sq km)
5 Lake Michigan, North America	22,300sq mi (57,800sq km)

WEATHER RECORDS

Hottest temperature:
136 °F (57.8 °C) at Al Aziziyah in Libya, in 1922.
Coldest temperature:
-128.6 °F (-89.2 °C) at Vostok Station, Antarctica, in 1983.

TOP FIVE ISLANDS

1 Greenland, Atlantic/Arctic Ocean	836,300sq mi (2,166,000sq km)
2 New Guinea, Pacific Ocean	309,000sq mi (800,000sq km)
3 Borneo, Indian Ocean	292,000sq mi (755,000sq km)
4 Madagascar, Indian Ocean	226,658sq mi (587,041sq km)
5 Baffin Island, Arctic Ocean	195,928sq mi (507,451sq km)

DID YOU KNOW?
The longest country in the world is Chile. It measures about 2,700mi (4,300km) from north to south.

THE HIGHEST MOUNTAINS

1 Mount Everest	The Nepal/China border, the Himalayas, Asia	29,035ft (8,850m)
2 K2 or Chogori	The Karakoram Range, the Himalayas, Asia	28,251ft (8,611m)
3 Kangchenjunga	The India/Nepal border, the Himalayas, Asia	28,169ft (8,586m)
4 Lhotse	The Nepal/China border, the Himalayas, Asia	27,890ft (8,501m)
5 Makalu	The Nepal/China border, the Himalayas, Asia	27,766ft (8,463 m)

MIGHTY VOLCANOES

Vesuvius, Italy	Last serious eruption, 1944 – destroyed the Roman town of Pompeii in AD79
Etna, Sicily, Italy	Killed at least 20,000 people in 1669
Krakatoa, Indonesia	The famous eruption of 1883 killed over 36,000 people
Mount St Helens, USA	Last serious eruption, 1980
Mont Pelée, Martinique, West Indies	An eruption in 1902 killed 26,000 people

BIGGEST DESERTS

Sahara Desert, Africa	more than 8.4 million sq km
Australian Desert	1.5 million sq km
Arabian Desert	1.3 million sq km
Gobi Desert, Asia	1 million sq km
Kalahari Desert, Africa	520,000 sq km

Note: figures based mainly on the US Census Bureau International Database and *Encyclopedia Britannica*.

DID YOU KNOW?
The Pacific is the deepest of the Earth's oceans. Its deepest point is 35,797ft (10,911m) down in the Marianas Trench.

GLOSSARY

Altitude Height above sea level.

Aztec civilization Empire of Mexico, at its peak in the 1400s, and ended by the Spanish conquest of 1521.

Berbers The non-Arab, indigenous (original) people of North Africa.

Bronze Age A period in ancient history from about 5000 BC, when people made tools of bronze (a metal alloy of copper and tin).

Conservationist Someone who works to protect the natural environment and its wildlife.

Delta A fan-shaped river mouth, with many branches, flowing into the sea.

Dependency A territory ruled by another country, similar to a colony.

Ecological niche The place within a community of living things occupied by each species. Ecology is the study of how all living things interact.

Equatorial zone The hot region of the Earth either side of the Equator. The equatorial zone has heavy rainfall, thunderstorms and only light winds.

Game reserve A wildlife park in which wild animals are protected from hunting and human interference.

Geographical north Also known as true north, it is the location of the North Pole. It does not move, unlike the magnetic North pole, which changes position.

Geyser A spouting eruption of hot water and steam from underground.

Glaciers Slow-moving 'rivers' of ice, flowing downhill in icy regions.

Global warming Temperature rises leading to climate change, believed by most scientists to be increased by burning fossil fuels (oil, coal and gas).

Grid location A way of showing the precise position of a place on a map, using letters and numbers on a grid (a pattern of squares).

Habitat The place where one community of animals and plants find the food and shelter they need.

Iberian peninsula A region in western Europe consisting of two countries: Spain and Portugal.

Immigrants People who have left their homeland and moved to another country to settle.

Inca civilization An ancient empire in the Andes of South America, conquered by Spain in the 1530s.

Industrial Revolution The age of factories, machines and new science processes that began in Britain in the 1700s and spread around the world.

Magnetic north The North magnetic pole, to which a compass needle always points.

Mayan civilization A Central American culture, at its height between AD 300 and 900.

Minoan civilization The first major civilization in Europe, based on the island of Crete. It was at its height from about 2000 to 1700 BC.

Moors People from North Africa who occupied southern Spain (711–1492).

Native Describes the indigenous (original) people or wildlife of a region, such as Native Americans.

Natural resources The riches of nature, such as soil, water, trees and minerals (often found in rocks).

Olmec civilization A culture of Mexico that flourished between 1200 and 300 BC.

Pampas The grassy plains of southern South America.

Plantation A large farm used for growing one crop, such as sugarcane, bananas or tea.

Projection Method of drawing a map to show as accurately as possible the parallels (lines) of latitude and the meridians (lines) of longitude, and the shape and sizes of the world's various land masses.

Savanna grasslands Grassy plains in Africa, noted for their vast herds of grazing animals.

Seven wonders of the ancient world Structures of ancient times that were the marvels of their age. Only the pyramids of Egypt survive.

Shanty slums Districts with ramshackle housing, and no drains or clean water. Such slums are often found on the outskirts of big cities.

Sub-continent A large part of a continent, with a distinctive character. The term is often used to describe India and Pakistan, in Asia.

Toltec civilization A civilization of Mexico that flourished between AD 900 and 1200.

INDEX

The entries in this index are to text references and do not include the maps in the book.